D1523490

THE RISE OF MAMMALS

THE PALEOCENE & EOCENE EPOCHS

THE PREHISTORIC EARTH

THE PREHISTORIC EARTH

THE RISE OF MAMMALS

THE PALEOCENE & EOCENE EPOCHS

Thom Holmes

CHELSEA HOUSE
PUBLISHERS
An imprint of Infobase Publishing

Chelsea House
An imprint of Infobase Publishing
132 West 31st Street
New York NY 10001

Library of Congress Cataloging-in-Publication Data

Holmes, Thom.
  Rise of the mammals : the Paleocene and Eocene epochs / Thom Holmes.
    p. cm. — (The prehistoric Earth)
  Includes bibliographical references and index.
  ISBN 978-0-8160-5963-8 (hardcover)
  1. Mammals, Fossil. 2. Mammals—Evolution. 3. Paleontology—Paleocene. 4. Paleontology—Eocene. I. Title.
  QE881.H75 2009
  569—dc22   2008038330

Chelsea House books are available at special discounts when purchased in bulk quantities for businesses, associations, institutions, or sales promotions. Please call our Special Sales Department in New York at (212) 967-8800 or (800) 322-8755.

You can find Chelsea House on the World Wide Web at http://www.chelseahouse.com

Text design by Kerry Casey
Cover design by Salvatore Luongo
Section opener images © John Sibbick

Printed in the United States of America

Bang NMSG 10 9 8 7 6 5 4 3 2 1

This book is printed on acid-free paper.

All links and Web addresses were checked and verified to be correct at the time of publication. Because of the dynamic nature of the Web, some addresses and links may have changed since publication and may no longer be valid.

CONTENTS

PREFACE

To be curious about the future, one must know something about the past.

Humans have been recording events in the world around them for about 5,300 years. That is how long it has been since the Sumerian people, in a land that is today part of southern Iraq, invented the first known written language. Writing allowed people to document what they saw happening around them. The written word gave a new permanency to life. Language, and writing in particular, made history possible.

History is a marvelous human invention, but how do people know about things that happened before language existed? Or before humans existed? Events that took place before human record keeping began are called *prehistory*. Prehistoric life is, by its definition, any life that existed before human beings existed and were able to record for posterity what was happening in the world around them.

Prehistory is as much a product of the human mind as history. Scientists who specialize in unraveling clues of prehistoric life are called *paleontologists*. They study life that existed before human history, often hundreds of thousands and millions, and even billions, of years in the past. Their primary clues come from fossils of animals, plants, and other organisms, as well as geologic evidence about the Earth's topography and climate. Through the skilled and often clever interpretation of fossils, paleontologists are able to reconstruct the appearances, lifestyles, environments, and relationships of ancient life-forms. While paleontology is grounded in a study of prehistoric life, it draws on many other sciences to complete an accurate picture of the past. Information from the fields of biology, zoology, geology, chemistry, meteorology, and even astrophysics is called into play to help the paleontologist view the past through the lens of today's knowledge.

If a writer were to write a history of all sports, would it be enough to write only about table tennis? Certainly not. On the shelves of bookstores and libraries, however, we find just such a slanted perspective toward the story of the dinosaurs. Dinosaurs have captured our imagination at the expense of many other equally fascinating, terrifying, and unusual creatures. Dinosaurs were not alone in the pantheon of prehistoric life, but it is rare to find a book that also mentions the many other kinds of life that came before and after the dinosaurs.

The Prehistoric Earth is a series that explores the evolution of life from its earliest forms 3.5 billion years ago until the emergence of modern humans about 300,000 years ago. Three volumes in the series trace the story of the dinosaurs. Seven other volumes are devoted to the kinds of animals that evolved before, during, and after the reign of the dinosaurs. *The Prehistoric Earth* covers the early explosion of life in the oceans; the invasion of the land by the first land animals; the rise of fishes, amphibians, reptiles, mammals, and birds; and the emergence of modern humans.

The Prehistoric Earth series is written for readers in high school and college. Based on the latest scientific findings in paleontology, *The Prehistoric Earth* is the most comprehensive and up-to-date series of its kind for this age group.

The first volume in the series, *Early Life*, offers foundational information about geologic time, Earth science, fossils, the classification of organisms, and evolution. This volume also begins the chronological exploration of fossil life that explodes with the incredible life-forms of Precambrian times and the Cambrian Period, more than 500 million years ago.

The remaining nine volumes in the series can be read chronologically. Each volume covers a specific geologic time period and describes the major forms of life that lived at that time. The books also trace the geologic forces and climate changes that affected the evolution of life through the ages. Readers of *The Prehistoric Earth* will see the whole picture of prehistoric life take shape. They will learn about forces that affect life on Earth, the directions that life can sometimes take, and ways in which all life-forms depend on each other in the environment. Along the way, readers also will meet many of the scientists who have made remarkable discoveries about the prehistoric Earth.

The language of science is used throughout this series, with ample definition and with an extensive glossary provided in each volume. Important concepts involving geology, evolution, and the lives of early animals are presented logically, step by step. Illustrations, photographs, tables, and maps reinforce and enhance the books' presentation of the story of prehistoric life.

While telling the story of prehistoric life, the author hopes that many readers will be sufficiently intrigued to continue studies on their own. For this purpose, throughout each volume, special "Think About It" sidebars offer additional insights or interesting exercises for readers who wish to explore certain topics. Each book in the series also provides a chapter-by-chapter bibliography of books, journals, and Web sites.

Only about one-tenth of 1 percent of all species of prehistoric animals are known from fossils. A multitude of discoveries remain to be made in the field of paleontology. It is with earnest, best wishes that I hope that some of these discoveries will be made by readers inspired by this series.

—Thom Holmes
Jersey City, New Jersey

ACKNOWLEDGMENTS

I would like to thank the many dedicated and hardworking people at Chelsea House. A special debt of gratitude goes to my editors, Shirley White, Justine Ciovacco, Lisa Rand, Brian Belval, and Frank Darmstadt, for their support and guidance in conceiving and making *The Prehistoric Earth* a reality. Frank was instrumental in fine-tuning the features of the series as well as accepting my ambitious plan for creating a comprehensive reference for students. Brian greatly influenced the development of the color illustration program and supported my efforts to integrate the work of some of the best artists in the field, most notably John Sibbick, whose work appears throughout the set. Shirley, Justine, and Lisa took the helm of the project when it entered the production stage and have been remarkable in shaping the text, the design, and the illustration program that you now see in the published volumes.

I am privileged to have worked with some of the brightest minds in paleontology on this series. Grégoire Métais, post-doctoral fellow of vertebrate paleontology at the Carnegie Museum of Natural History in Pittsburgh (now of the Muséum National d'Histoire Naturelle in Paris), reviewed the draft of *The Rise of Mammals* and made many important suggestions that affected the course of the work. Grégoire also wrote the Foreword for the volume.

The excellent copyediting of Mary Ellen Kelly was both thoughtful and vital to shaping the final manuscript, and I thank her for her valuable review and suggestions.

In many ways, a set of books such as this requires years of preparation. Some of the work is educational, and I owe much gratitude to Dr. Peter Dodson of the University of Pennsylvania for his gracious and inspiring tutelage over the years. Another dimension of preparation requires experience digging fossils, and for giving me these opportunities I thank my friends and colleagues who have taken me into the field with them, including Phil Currie, Rodolfo Coria, Matthew Lammana, and Rubén Martínez. Finally comes the work needed to put thoughts down on paper and complete the draft of a book, a process that always takes many more hours than I plan on. I thank Anne for bearing with my constant state of busy-ness and for helping me remember the important things in life. You are an inspiration to me. I also thank my daughter, Shaina, the genius in the family and another inspiration, for always being supportive and humoring her father's obsession with prehistoric life.

FOREWORD

Mammals are among the most successful animals on earth. They occupy every major habitat, from the equator to the poles, on land, underground, in the air, in the trees, and in both fresh and salt waters. They have colonized diverse dietary niches, and they move about by means of varied locomotor systems closely related to their wide-ranging sizes—from about 3 grams for the bumblebee bat to over 100 tons for the blue whale.

The great majority of what we know about the evolutionary history of mammals is from the Cenozoic Era—the "Age of Mammals"—that represents only the last one-third of mammalian history. The Paleocene Epoch constitutes the base of the Cenozoic and encompasses the 10 million years that followed the mass extinctions at the end of the Cretaceous. The uninhabited ecospaces left by the disappearance of non-avian dinosaurs offered the conditions for what often is described as the "explosive" radiation of mammals. Mammals coexisted with dinosaurs during the first two-thirds of mammalian history, but the fossil record documents an extensive and relatively rapid adaptive radiation during the Paleocene and the Early Eocene. Nearly all the modern mammal groups, as well as many extinct groups, first appear during this time period, between 65 and 50 million years ago.

This series of books, *The Prehistoric Earth*, offers an outstanding account of the history that led to Earth's modern biodiversity. This book, *The Rise of Mammals*, particularly examines the early history of Cenozoic mammals and offers an extensive review of mammal groups, now extinct, that lived on Earth just after the famous mass extinctions that characterized the end of the Cretaceous. If you are not already familiar with these weird mammals, you will find here a state-of-the-art review of the current understanding of their morphology, supposed habits, and relationships with modern groups of mammals.

This book not only provides an extensive and detailed review of extinct forms that lived on Earth during the Paleocene, but also shows how abiotic factors such as climate and geography contributed to shaping the extant picture of mammal diversity and biogeography. For example, the Paleocene-Eocene boundary, 55.8 million years ago, is marked by a rapid and important global warming that certainly affected the course of mammalian evolution. That time saw the appearance of several modern mammal groups whose rise appears to be directly related to this dramatic climatic shift.

Ours is an exciting time in which to learn about paleontology. There are many new discoveries from throughout geologic time, new interpretations of previously studied fossils, and new approaches for extracting more information from the fossil record. Fossils not only provide irrefutable evidence of evolution, they also offer data critical to our understanding of the mechanisms and tempo of evolution. Likewise, studies of the geological context of fossil beds contribute to a refining of our understanding of the paleoenvironmental, ecological, and temporal framework for the history of life.

The Prehistoric Earth of Thom Holmes offers readers a fantastic trip through geologic time. We primates certainly have much to learn from this long and still continuing history. Enjoy reading this volume of *The Prehistoric Earth,* and keep the big ideas from *The Rise of Mammals* with you as you continue to learn about the history of life on Earth in the other books in the series.

—Dr. Grégoire Métais
Muséum National d'Histoire Naturelle
UMR 5143 du CNRS
Paris, France

INTRODUCTION

The story of the **evolution** of the **dinosaurs** was concluded in *Last of the Dinosaurs*, the previous volume in this series. Living in the shadow of the dinosaurs were two key vertebrate orders that came into their own after the **mass extinction** that eradicated the lords of the Mesozoic **Era.** The birds and the mammals inherited an Earth in upheaval and found new niches in which to expand. They became the most prominent terrestrial vertebrates of the last 60 million years. Thus continues the story of vertebrate evolution in the Cenozoic Era, the new age of life detailed in *The Rise of Mammals.*

The story continues by unraveling the early evolution and radiation of mammals and birds, survivors of the Mesozoic Era. The patterns of bird and mammal evolution prior to the Cenozoic are recounted, as are the patterns of bird and mammal evolution in the critical first 10 million-year span of the Cenozoic known as the Paleocene Epoch. The Paleocene was a time of recovery for mammals and birds, followed by their rapid adaptation to new ecological conditions. The face of Earth continued to change as the continents drifted farther apart. This eventually isolated certain **fauna**, such as those of the southern continents, where life took its own, often singularly peculiar, evolutionary path. It was a world of evolutionary experiments, as birds and mammals each found ways to fill the ecological gaps left vacant by the disappearance of the dinosaurs. By the end of the Paleocene, the roots of most modern birds and mammal families had been set, forging a series of divergent and specialized paths that continue to radiate about 55 million years later.

OVERVIEW OF *THE RISE OF MAMMALS*

The Rise of Mammals begins by looking at the geological and ecological conditions that created opportunities for the expansion of the mammals and birds of the Cenozoic Era. Chapter 1 assesses the damage done by the mass-extinction event that killed the dinosaurs and tells how the world's habitats changed soon thereafter. The story of the Cenozoic is also one of changing continental barriers and locations, all of which affected habitats and ranges for terrestrial animals.

The evolution of modern bird families is traced in Chapter 2. The **anatomy** of birds is explored, as are differences between modern birds and their Mesozoic Era kin. Families of modern birds are defined, and specific **taxa** of extinct Cenozoic birds are introduced; these range from the giant, flightless predatory birds of 50 million years ago to such recently extinct **species** as the dodo.

Early mammals are explored in Chapter 3. The Mesozoic roots of the mammal family tree are outlined, as are the biological traits that make up the modern definition of *mammal*. The extensive categories of modern mammal groups are explained in Chapter 4, thus providing a blueprint for putting specific taxa of extinct and living mammals in perspective.

Chapter 5, "Conquest of the Mammals," takes a close look at the earliest mammals of the Cenozoic, the animals that formed the foundation of all modern lines of mammals. The Paleocene Epoch was not only a time of increasing diversity in mammals, but also a time during which the first modern mammals began to replace many archaic lines of ancestral mammals.

The Conclusion of *The Rise of Mammals* recaps the evolutionary milestones that led to the success of modern mammals, thereby providing a framework from which to jump into another volume of *The Prehistoric Earth: The Age of Mammals.*

Each chapter uses an abundance of tables, maps, figures, and photos to depict the conditions, habitats, and changing evolutionary patterns that affected the lives of the vertebrates. Two chapters also include "Think About It" sidebars that focus on interesting issues, people, history, and discoveries related to Cenozoic life.

The Rise of Mammals builds on the same foundational principles of geology, **fossils**, and the study of life that are introduced in other volumes of *The Prehistoric Earth*. Readers who want to refresh their knowledge of certain basic terms and principles in the study of past life may wish to consult the Glossary in the back of *The Rise of Mammals*. Perhaps most important to keep in mind are the basic rules governing evolution: that the process of evolution is set in motion first by the traits inherited by individuals and then by the interaction of a population of a species with those traits with its habitat. Changes that enable the population to survive accumulate generation after generation, often producing and allowing species to adapt to changing conditions in the world around them. As Charles Darwin (1809–1882) explained, "The small differences distinguishing varieties of the same species steadily tend to increase, till they equal the greater differences between species of the same genus, or even of distinct **genera**." These are the rules of nature that served to stoke the engine of evolution during the Paleozoic since the appearance of life on Earth, giving rise to forms of life whose descendants still populate Earth.

SECTION ONE:
THE WORLD OF
THE MAMMALS

1

THE CENOZOIC ERA

The Cenozoic Era is the era of "new life." It includes the most recent, and current, of the three traditional divisions of geologic time that encompass the span of life on Earth. The Cenozoic began 65.5 million years ago, following the mass-extinction event that marked the end of the Mesozoic Era. The Cenozoic Era is also known as the Age of Mammals because it has been during the past 65.5 million years that mammals have become the dominant form of life on Earth They have diversified in remarkable ways and represent the most adaptable examples of vertebrate evolution.

In terms of longevity, modern humans appear late in the Cenozoic—a mere 2 million to 3 million years ago—representing an escalating reign of mammals species that had earlier radiated to all corners of the planet. Prior to humans, the world was ruled by a wide assortment of mammals of many kinds: **carnivorous**, herbivorous, terrestrial, and marine.

Birds, the last surviving members of the dinosaur family line, also diversified and radiated widely during the Cenozoic but never achieved the ecological dominance of their dinosaurian ancestors. This chapter outlines the geologic and climatic events that influenced the evolution and diversification of mammals during the past 65 million years and presents a framework of time periods and epochs for the discussion of mammal evolution.

THE K-T EXTINCTION: LOSERS AND WINNERS

A rapid change to Earth habitats that kills a significant number of species is called a mass extinction. Mass extinctions are devastating to life and mark points in the geological record at which previously dominant life-forms entirely disappear. Chief among the causes of mass extinction are brutal environmental changes that affect the food supply or body chemistry of organisms; disease; and natural disasters such as volcanic eruptions, earthquakes, and the impact of meteorites.

Mass extinctions may have many causes; often, they are the result of multiple, accumulating natural disasters. Even mass extinctions take a long time to unravel Earth's ecosystem, however—perhaps as long as a million years in some cases. The causes of mass extinctions are not always as sudden as one might first think, but they generally involve a widespread change to the environment triggered by changes in average global temperature, sea levels, and shifts in the shape, configuration, and geographic location of landmasses.

The worst mass extinction of all time climaxed 251 million years ago, at the end of the Permian **Period**, which marks the last of the Paleozoic Era. The **extinction** was triggered by a prolonged period of massive volcanic eruptions that lasted several hundred thousand years. Enormous flows of lava, centered in what today is Siberia, probably caused global warming and a runaway greenhouse effect that lasted thousands of years. This in turn caused **climate** changes that affected plant and animal life on land and in the sea. There also were dramatic shifts in Earth's crust during this period; these shifts affected ocean levels and the habitats of all organisms. This mass extinction exterminated about 95 percent of marine plant and animal species and 75 percent of terrestrial species. By comparison, the Cretaceous-Tertiary (**K-T**) **extinction**, which included the dinosaurs among its victims, killed between 65 percent and 75 percent of the world's species of plants and animals.

The last of the dinosaurs, pterosaurs, and Mesozoic marine reptiles became extinct 65.5 million years ago in the K-T extinction. This marked a division in time between the Cretaceous (*kreta* is Latin for chalk) Period and the Paleogene Period that marks the onset of the Cenozoic Era. *Tertiary* is the historical name given to the first geologic period following the start of the Cretaceous, and it is known now as the Paleocene Epoch. The K-T event was a mass extinction, wiping out about 65 percent to 75 percent of all plant and animal species in the world's biota—its **flora** and fauna. Even those groups of organisms that survived—including frogs, lizards, turtles, salamanders, birds, insects, fish, crocodiles, alligators, mammals, other invertebrates, and plants—lost great numbers of their species.

The fame of the K-T extinction is due to the cast of characters that were affected. It was the end of the "Age of Reptiles," dominated by the dinosaurs, and the beginning of "the Age of Mammals," the time during which early mammals diversified and radiated across the planet, eventually leading to the evolution of primates and humans, including the order of primates to which humans belong.

Mammals existed before the K-T extinction; they have roots in the Triassic Period, during the rise of the dinosaurs. The diversity of Mesozoic mammals remains poorly known, but recent research shows a relative morphological and ecological diversity among Mesozoic mammals. They were ecologically limited by the presence of the dominant dinosaurs, however. The mammals lived in the dinosaurs' shadows and never grew very large.

The extraordinary natural events leading to the rise of the mammals are not entirely understood, but theories abound as to why mammals suddenly found success in the early part of the Cenozoic Era. These ideas are explored in Chapter 3, "Early Mammals."

The K-T Extinction: A Combination of Causes

Many causes have been asserted as culprits behind the K-T extinction. Of these, there is one certainty on which most scientists agree: Very close to 65 million years ago, a large bolide from outer space—variously described as a wayward comet, a meteor, or an asteroid—struck Earth in an area located on the northern perimeter of the Yucatán Peninsula, in Mexico. This idea was first suggested in 1980 by a research team led by Nobel Prize–winning physicist Luis Alvarez (1911–1988) and his geologist son Walter Alvarez (b. 1940), at the University of California, Berkeley.

While studying stratigraphic layers in Italy, the Alvarez team noticed a thin, barely noticeable layer of clay deposited about 65.5 million years ago. Analysis of the clay revealed that it contained 30 times the concentration of the mineral iridium than is normally found in layers of the Earth. Knowing that such high levels of iridium have also been found in asteroids, the Alvarez team theorized that the deposit was the result of a severe collision of Earth with an asteroid. The Alvarez finding has since been corroborated by the discovery of many other locations around the Earth that feature high concentrations of iridium dating from the end of the Cretaceous Period. The fact that this suspected asteroid hit coincided with the mass extinction of the dinosaurs made the theory that much more intriguing.

The mechanism behind the asteroid strike and subsequent mass extinction began when the impact thrust a great cloud of dust into the atmosphere. That cloud quickly circled the globe. Initially, the cloud of smoke and dust was incendiary: It was full of burning ash and set fires worldwide. It also blocked sunlight for weeks or months. The result was a gradual diminishment of plant life and the gradual deaths of organisms that fed on plants and **predators** that fed on the plant eaters.

A related breakthrough in support of the Alvarez impact theory came in 1990. Graduate geology student Alan R. Hildebrand (b. 1955) was exploring rock layers in Haiti and the Yucatán Peninsula for evidence of ancient tsunamis. After he found quantities of iridium, shocked quartz (quartz with a crystalline structure that has been deformed by intense pressure), and tektites (natural glass formed by the impact of large meteorites) at various locations in the area, Hildebrand turned his attention to the idea that an impact crater was located in the region. A petroleum engineer named Glen T. Penfield had come to a similar conclusion about 10 years earlier, while investigating the makeup of oil drill cores from the Yucatan. Backed by Penfield's earlier findings, Hildebrand announced in 1991 that he had identified the most likely candidate for the "crater of doom" that led to the demise of the dinosaurs. Now called the

Chicxulub crater for a nearby town, the Mexican crater measures 283 miles (170 km) in diameter. The asteroid that caused this crater was about six miles (10 km) across. Another asteroid or comet may have struck Earth at about the same time, but the location of that strike's crater is still in dispute.

Despite this dramatic and catastrophic geologic event, there is evidence that many Mesozoic organisms had become extinct or were beginning the downward spiral toward extinction long before the collision of Earth with a bolide. There is evidence of a cooling trend during the last few million years of the Cretaceous that resulted in moderating climates and a fall in sea temperature. There also was a long period of volcanic flood-lava eruptions; these eruptions formed the Deccan Traps in west-central India, one of the most expansive volcanic features on the surface of Earth. The Deccan Traps now compose a layer of igneous rock that is more than 6,600 feet (2,000 m) thick in some locations and that spreads over an area of more than 200,000 square miles (518,000 square km).

Dated to within the last half-million years of the Cretaceous, these eruptions may have lasted 30,000 years, spewing volcanic ash and a rush of carbon dioxide into the atmosphere. The ash would have caused global cooling, and the carbon dioxide may have affected the life-giving balance of oceanic chemistry. The bottom line is that the land and the oceans were getting cooler, and the mixture of life-sustaining chemicals in the air and water was recombining in ways that could have affected many kinds of organisms, from the smallest algae and plankton in the seas to land plants and the creatures that fed on them. It was a very tenuous time for life on Earth.

The timing of the final blows that led to the extinction of the last of the dinosaurs is a matter of debate. One theory, advanced by geoscientist Gerta Keller (b. 1945) of Princeton University, is that Earth was bombarded by multiple asteroids during a 300,000-year span leading up to the end of the Cretaceous Period. In Keller's opinion, those asteroid strikes combined with the calamitous volcanic activity of the Deccan Traps to bring life nearly to a halt over much of the planet.

The K-T extinction was possibly capped by the strike of a large asteroid.

In 2006, geologist Ken MacLeod of the University of Missouri-Columbia suggested that the K-T extinction was more sudden. He based his results on deep-ocean sediments from five locations in the Atlantic Ocean that showed, in MacLeod's opinion, a narrow depositional layer of impact-related material that was laid down following an enormous asteroid strike that was sudden and conclusive. "One shot, and that's all you need to explain it," declared MacLeod. Keller's team says that the jury is still out until additional, verifiable evidence can be agreed on for a single- or multiple-impact scenario.

CHANGING CLIMATES AND HABITATS OF THE CENOZOIC EARTH

Most of the familiar features of the modern landscape took shape during the Cenozoic Era. The current configuration of the continents took shape rapidly by geologic standards. The breakup of **Pangaea** was completed, thus forming more clearly divided continents in the Northern and Southern Hemispheres. The movement and collisions of Earth's crustal plates resulted in a hyperactive period of mountain building that continues today. In North America, the Appalachian Mountains—which began the Cenozoic as a highly eroded flat plain—were lifted up, as tectonic stresses pressed the area's ancient bedrock together, forcing it upward. The Rocky Mountains were uplifted to their present height as a widening Atlantic Ocean pressed westward, transferring the stresses of its expansion inland. The Alps in Europe and the Himalayas in Central Asia were uplifted by collisions of Africa and Turkey with Europe to the west and Asia with India, Arabia, and Thailand in the east.

Tectonic-plate movements during the Cenozoic dried up a vast but shallow inland sea in North America. The Tethys Sea, a shallow ocean that covered much of Europe during the late Mesozoic, was displaced by colliding landmasses. What was once the Tethys Sea is today occupied by India, Indonesia, and the Indian Ocean. The only watery remnants of this body of water are the Black, Caspian, and Aral Seas in Asia.

The formation of all of today's continents took place during the late Mesozoic and the Cenozoic Eras. Australia and New Guinea broke from **Gondwana** and drifted north. India broke apart from the Antarctic landmass and drifted north to become part of Central Asia. Antarctica assumed its present position over the South Pole. South America, having already detached from Africa, broke its land

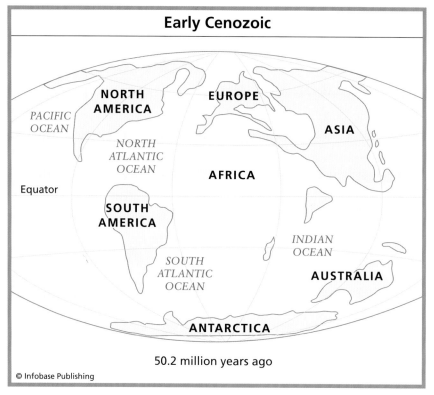

Early Cenozoic

NORTH
AMERICA

EUROPE

PACIFIC
OCEAN

ASIA

NORTH
ATLANTIC
OCEAN

AFRICA

Equator

SOUTH
AMERICA

INDIAN
OCEAN

SOUTH
ATLANTIC
OCEAN

AUSTRALIA

ANTARCTICA

50.2 million years ago

© Infobase Publishing

The geologic positioning of the major continents during the early part of the
Cenozoic Era was much like it is today.

link to Antarctica but developed a bridge to Central and North
America.

Important for the study of vertebrate evolution were the isolation of flora and fauna on the continents of Australia and South
America. Each continent became isolated during the Cenozoic. This
resulted in the development of unique variations of vertebrates that
differed from those seen in Africa and in the Northern Hemisphere
landmasses that maintained land bridges that allowed the radiation
of fauna over a wider geographic range.

The climate of the early Cenozoic continued the warm, greenhouse trend that began in the Late Cretaceous Epoch. Earth was
so warm that crocodiles and plants associated with temperate

climates lived near the Arctic Circle. The break of Australia and South America from Antarctica drastically modified the circulation of air and seas in the Southern Hemisphere, however, and trapped cold air over the South Pole. This caused Antarctic glaciation. In turn, a period of global cooling devastated once-tropical forests and many of the flora and fauna that lived there. Continued cooling of the globe led to the establishment of widespread grassy plains, or savannas, in North America, Europe, and Central Asia. In Europe, the Mediterranean Sea experienced repeated drying events, which drastically affected savanna life in that part of the world.

Ice Ages

A final stage in the development of Cenozoic climate led to the **ice ages**, which began about 4 million years ago. Ice ages are periodic spans of cooling that result in the development of ice sheets, or glaciers, that extend from the poles. During the later Cenozoic, ice caps formed on both poles, and glaciers began to reach into the adjacent continents, especially in the Northern Hemisphere. The ice advanced and receded four different times during the past 4 million years; it covered nearly one-third of the land surface of Earth during each episode. The spans between such intense periods of glaciation—spans during which Earth warms temporarily, and the ice recedes—are called interglacial periods. The last ice age peaked about 10,000 years ago, and we currently are experiencing an interglacial period.

The reasons for such an intense period of glaciation are not entirely understood, but several plausible causes, acting together or acting alone, all could have influenced the development of massive ice sheets:

Variations in Earth's orbit and inclination. The angle at which sunlight strikes any portion of Earth affects the degree of solar radiation that is absorbed. The natural fluctuation, or wobble, of Earth's orbit over time is a major contributing factor to the appearance of glaciers, but that factor alone does not explain why this has not always been the case in the history of the planet. Other forces, such as the following, also must be taken into consideration.

Atmospheric changes. Fluctuations in the amount of carbon dioxide in the air can affect the amount of heat that is trapped by the atmosphere. When more carbon dioxide is present, more heat is trapped. Lesser amounts of carbon dioxide can lead to the escape of heat into the atmosphere. An offsetting effect is caused by volcanic eruptions that spew dust and other gases into the air, blocking sunlight and causing widespread cooling.

Continental movements and ocean currents. The shifting position of continental landmasses can affect global temperature, especially when landmasses congregate over the poles, thereby preventing ocean circulation and trapping cold air. The gradual movement of continents in the Northern Hemisphere toward the North Pole probably has contributed to glaciation.

Glaciation greatly affects the lives of flora and fauna. Fossils help to track the migration of species, particularly mammals, that advanced and retreated along with the harsh, glacial climates. When ice sheets reached down into areas now known as Wisconsin and New England, wooly mammoths, musk oxen, and reindeer made those places home. In Europe, arctic foxes, wooly mammoths, and reindeer ranged widely across the lower latitudes to escape the extensive tundra that encroached upon their northerly habitat. The teeth of mammoths and mastodons, members of the elephant family, have been found along the northeastern coast of North America; this attests to their abundance during a time of escape from the advancing glaciers.

Fossil evidence also shows that some interglacial periods were warmer than the current one. Plant and animal fossils found in southern Europe suggest a warmer climate during one such period, between 4,000 and 6,000 years ago: The fossils found include those of ancestral lions and hippopotamuses.

TIME AND GEOLOGIC DIVISIONS OF THE CENOZOIC

The Cenozoic Era covers about 65 million years, from the time of the extinction of the dinosaurs to the present day. The Cenozoic is divided into two periods, beginning with the Paleogene (65.5 million to

EVOLUTIONARY MILESTONES OF THE CENOZOIC ERA

Period	Epoch	Span (millions of years ago)	Organismal Milestones
Paleogene	Paleocene	65.5 to 55.8 mya	Radiation of flowering plants; diversification of marsupials; rise of eutherian mammals; diversification of birds
	Eocene	55.8 to 33.9 mya	Rise of primates, rodents, carnivores, rhinoceroses, early whales; diversification of Australian mammals
	Oligocene	33.9 to 23.03 mya	Rise of baleen and toothed whales and brontotheres; rise of elephants, camels, hippopotamuses, horses, and saber-toothed cats
Neogene	Miocene	23.03 to 5.33 mya	Radiation of grasses; diversification of South American mammals
	Pliocene	5.33 to 1.81 mya	Rise of deer, giraffes, and cattle; early hominids
Ice ages begin			
	Pleistocene	1.81 mya to 10,000 years ago	Rise of the genus *Homo*; rise of sloths, glyptodonts, bears, and dogs
	Holocene	10,000 years ago to present	Dominance of *Homo sapiens*

23 million years ago) and continuing with the Neogene (23 million years ago to the present). These periods are further divided into epochs, as shown in the accompanying table. The names of epochs will be used in *The Rise of Mammals* to indicate the times during which given organisms lived. The table also shows which major lines of vertebrates arose during given epochs.

Note that the terms *Paleogene* and *Neogene* currently are recommended by the International Commission on Stratigraphy to describe the time divisions of the Cenozoic Era. These terms replaced previously used terms—*Tertiary* and *Quaternary*—that remain historically important but that were dropped from formal stratigraphic nomenclature because of disagreement over how best to define them.

A NEW BEGINNING

Discussion of the K-T mass extinction naturally brings to mind the disappearance of previously dominant vertebrates such as the dinosaurs, pterosaurs, marine reptiles, and even freshwater sharks. The other intriguing story of this extinction concerns those creatures that survived because it was they that formed the biological basis for the animal kingdom that survives to this day.

Fossil records bridging the K-T gap show that among the survivors, birds and **marsupial** mammals were hard hit, losing about 75 percent of their families. Snakes, lizards, amphibians, turtles, fishes, and crocodiles were more fortunate, losing, on average, less than 17 percent of their families. Eutherian (placental) mammals also were more fortunate than their marsupial cousins, losing only 14 percent of their families.

So it was that mammals and other survivors entered the Cenozoic Era with the playing field of survival figuratively leveled by the extinction of the dinosaurs and almost literally leveled by the collision of planet Earth with a giant meteor. Of all the survivors, mammals and birds appear to have been the quickest to adapt; both groups diversified rapidly. The story of these early adapters of the Cenozoic is related in the remaining chapters of *The Rise of Mammals*.

SUMMARY

This chapter outlined the geologic and climatic events that influenced the evolution and diversification of mammals during the past 65 million years and presented a framework of time periods and epochs for the discussion of mammal evolution.

1. The Cenozoic Era is the era of "new life"; it includes the most recent, and current, of the three traditional divisions of geologic time that began 65.5 million years ago. The Cenozoic Era is also known as the Age of Mammals; the era is made up of the Paleogene and Neogene Periods, which are divided further into the following epochs: the Paleocene, the Eocene, the Oligocene, the Miocene, the Pliocene, the Pleistocene, and the current epoch, the Holocene.

2. The last of the dinosaurs, pterosaurs, and Mesozoic marine reptiles became extinct 65.5 million years ago, at a point in time that geologists call the K-T extinction. This mass extinction marks a division in time between the Cretaceous (*kreta* in Latin) and Tertiary Periods. Tertiary is the former, historical name given to the first geologic period following the Cretaceous; the Tertiary is known now as the Paleogene Period.

3. The K-T extinction appears to have been caused by several natural disasters that affected life. These included a cooling trend during the last few million years of the Cretaceous that resulted in moderating climates and a fall in sea temperature. There was significant and sustained volcanic activity in the area of India known as the Deccan Traps during the last half-million years of the Cretaceous. Finally, Earth collided with a large asteroid close to the end of the Cretaceous Period, effectively drawing the final curtain on many forms of Mesozoic life.

4. The current configuration of the continents took shape during the Cenozoic Era; this completed the breakup of Pangaea and formed more clearly divided continents in the Northern and Southern Hemispheres.

5. The climate of the early Cenozoic continued the warm, greenhouse trend than began in the Late Cretaceous Epoch.

6. The separation of Australia and South America from Antarctica drastically modified the circulation of air and the seas in the Southern Hemisphere, trapping cold air over the South Pole and causing Antarctic glaciation (about 35 million years ago).

7. Ice ages are periodic spans of cooling that result in the development of ice sheets, or glaciers, that extend from the poles. During the later Cenozoic, ice caps formed on both poles, and glaciers began to reach into the adjacent continents, especially in the Northern Hemisphere.

8. Ice ages are caused by variations in Earth's orbit and inclination toward the Sun; by atmospheric changes such as fluctuating amounts of carbon dioxide—a gas that, when reduced, allows heat to escape from the atmosphere; by continental movements; and by ocean currents.

9. Of all of the survivors of the K-T extinction, mammals and birds appear to have been the most adaptable and diversified rapidly.

SECTION TWO:
EVOLUTION OF
MODERN BIRDS

THE BIRDS DIVERSIFY

The ancestors of birds and their dinosaur cousins were **archosaurian** reptiles. The first birds evolved from small, flightless **theropod** dinosaurs during the Middle and Late Jurassic Epochs. *Archaeopteryx* represents the first true bird that is known from the fossil record; it dates from about 145 million years ago. Even though *Archaeopteryx* was found in Germany, the Late Jurassic fossil record for birds is much too spotty to rule out the possibility that birds may have evolved first elsewhere. There is a gap of about 25 million years between *Archaeopteryx* and the next abundant fossil evidence of early birds. This fossil gap clouds the story of the early evolution of birds and makes it difficult to link *Archaeopteryx* to the many well-established families of birds that existed in the Early Cretaceous Epoch. Finding specimens of birds that existed just before and after *Archaeopteryx* remains one of the most intriguing challenges to **paleontologists**.

The fossil record for birds of the Cretaceous Period includes about 100 known species but is punctuated by considerable gaps, especially from about 115 million to 70 million years ago—an important span in the radiation of birds for which very little fossil evidence is currently known. The Cretaceous record of fossil birds is also geographically biased toward the Northern Hemisphere, where nearly 80 percent of **basal** bird species have been found. Asia currently is the focus of much fieldwork on fossil birds. More than half of the known species, sometimes represented by hundreds of specimens, have been found in China and Mongolia. One should not interpret this to mean that birds did not venture and thrive south of

Archaeopteryx, the first known bird.

the equator. As flying creatures, birds had extraordinary access to virtually any terrestrial environment on the globe. The geographic distribution of basal birds during the Cretaceous Period is merely subject to **bias** in the fossil record: No fossil deposits of the right age equate to no record of birds. Pockets of excellent bird fossils have been found in Madagascar and Argentina, attesting to the fact that birds did indeed radiate southward in great numbers.

Mesozoic birds lived in the shadows of the dinosaurs and the large, flying reptiles known as pterosaurs, quietly adapting to a variety of habitats during the latter stage of the Cretaceous Period. Birds

Early birds were part of a diverse ecosystem in China during the Early Cretaceous Epoch that was also populated by dinosaurs and mammals.

still share many anatomical features that first appeared in their **non-avian** dinosaur brethren. These include hollow limb bones; feathers; a sternum (the wish bone); and three-toed feet—all features that were developed for reasons not associated with flight.

Sometime during the Middle Jurassic Epoch, prior to the appearance of *Archaeopteryx*, it is theorized, one or more lines of small maniraptoran dinosaurs began to exhibit changes to the anatomy of their **forelimbs** that led to the development of winged flight. The most widely accepted scenario is that the lengthening of the forelimbs and other anatomical changes needed to flap the wings were the natural extension of the reach-and-grab gesture that these small dinosaurs used to chase down prey. This gesture is sometimes called the predatory stroke. It can be seen in the fossil record of maniraptoran dinosaurs as a gradual change in an increasingly sideways rotation of the wrist, in the orientation of the shoulder socket, and in modification of the digits.

The small, bipedal dinosaur ancestors of birds probably were feathered, lightweight, and fast runners. Running and jumping to catch small prey such as flying insects or dodging the charges of larger predatory dinosaurs would have required good speed and maneuverability. Prior to the evolution of fully functional flight wings, feathered forelimbs with clawed hands would have improved the ability of these small dinosaurs to grasp or trap small prey. Such forelimbs also could have served as primitive air foils to cushion, bank, and improve the maneuverability of the animal as it ran and leaped. Maniraptorans exhibiting these inherited traits passed them along to their offspring.

Over many generations, continued changes to the forelimbs eventually led to the appearance of stronger, broader, and fully formed wings for powered flight, an innovation so successful that it greatly improved the ability of these early birds to hunt and to escape from being hunted. Those maniraptorans that developed wings became the foundation of the **clade** Aves, or birds. The story of the evolution of early birds in the Mesozoic Era is told in another book in this series, *Last of the Dinosaurs.*

Following the K-T extinction and the removal of dinosaurs and pterosaurs from the evolutionary story, birds began to diversify and radiate rapidly. There currently are about 9,100 species of living birds, in 153 families, plus an additional 77 known groups of extinct birds. Most of these modern bird groups arose during the Cenozoic Era. This chapter explores the remarkable success of birds during the Cenozoic and describes some of the most remarkable extinct members of the **taxon**.

NEORNITHES: THE MODERN BIRDS

Modern birds are classified as Neornithes ("new birds") and are divided into two subgroups, the **Paleognathae**, or flightless birds, and the **Neognathae**, the huge group that includes the majority of living birds. Before examining the major kinds of birds found in these groups, and their extinct ancestors, it is worth noting that the origins of modern bird groups are a hotly contested issue in paleontology circles.

Prior to the Cenozoic Era and the K-T extinction, Enantiornithes, the "opposite birds," were the most diverse and geographically widespread early birds. Anatomically, the enantiornithine birds were closer to modern birds than to *Archaeopteryx* but still retained many primitive features. The name "opposite birds" was given to the group by paleontologist C.A. Walker in 1981 to describe the fusion of bones in the feet of this group. Rather than having ankle bones that are fused together from the middle bones to the outward bones, as in modern birds, the ankle bones of Enantiornithes were joined together in the opposite direction, from the ankle to the toes. As members of a group that consisted of more than 40 species, typical enantiornithines have been found in deposits that once were freshwater shore habitats. Enantiornithines ranged in size from birds that were the size of a wren or sparrow, such as *Sinornis* (Early Cretaceous, China), to *Enantiornis* (Late Cretaceous, Argentina), a bird about the size of an eagle. Most Enantiornithes were toothed, but a few, such as *Gobipteryx* (Late Cretaceous, Mongolia), had a toothless beak.

The Enantiornithes and several other groups of Mesozoic birds (described in *Last of the Dinosaurs*) became extinct at the end of the Cretaceous along with the dinosaurs. Other bird groups that have no known descendants beyond the K-T extinction include the Archaeopterygiformes, including the first bird, *Archaeopteryx* (Late Jurassic, Germany); the Confuciusornithiformes, a clade of toothless, crow-sized birds such as *Confuciusornis* (Early Cretaceous, China); the Hesperornithiformes, a group of large, flightless, and toothed diving sea birds that included *Hesperornis* (Late Cretaceous, Kansas, Nebraska, Alberta, and Manitoba); and the Ichthyornithiformes, a group of flying, toothed sea birds such as *Ichthyornis* (Late Cretaceous, Kansas, Texas, and Alabama).

The Origin and Rise of Modern Birds

Until recently, it was widely accepted that all groups of modern, **extant** birds arose during the Cenozoic Era, during which they exploded in diversity and number and became geographically widespread to fill the ecological niches vacated by the extinction of the dinosaurs and pterosaurs at the K-T extinction. The study of bird evolution has used the K-T extinction as an important dividing line between older, basal families of birds and their modern counterparts. A scarcity of Mesozoic bird fossils has made it difficult to think otherwise because so few clues have been available to directly link Mesozoic and Cenozoic bird families. No one disagrees that modern birds are the descendants of Mesozoic birds, but precisely where those links were made is not yet fully known.

Scientists working in two continuing lines of research have shed new light on the origins of modern birds and have concluded that some lines of Neornithes did indeed have roots in the Cretaceous. In 1996, a team of researchers led by biologist S. Blair Hedges of Pennsylvania State University used the technique of **molecular time estimation** to push back the origin of modern birds to the Early Cretaceous Epoch. Hedges explains that molecular time estimation uses the "clock-like accumulation of sequence differences in some **genes**" to count back in time to estimate the points at which some inherited traits may have originated.

The process of molecular time estimation begins with a known gene sequence and counts backward, but the process cannot account for possible changes in the pace of evolution that may have been caused by such things as mass extinctions. Despite this, the Hedges team made a compelling case and suggested that the rapid diversification and radiation of modern bird groups known from the Cenozoic began much earlier, as far back as the Early Cretaceous Epoch. This time estimation infers that the expansion of modern bird families was more gradual than is traditionally thought and not directly related, at first, to the K-T extinction; the evolution of many preexisting bird families also could have accelerated rapidly following the demise of the dinosaurs, however.

As an alternative hypothesis for the rapid radiation of birds, Hedges proposed that the expansion of birds instead was necessitated by the breakup of Pangaea during the Cretaceous Period. That breakup would have been a leading mechanism in the diversification of early bird groups because they were isolated on increasingly wide-spread landmasses.

Continuing work with molecular time estimates by Hedges and others provides somewhat conflicting results, but the bottom line is generally the same: The roots of modern bird groups appear to extend back to the middle part of the Cretaceous Period, between 115 million and 65.5 million years ago.

A second line of evidence for the origins of the Neornithes comes from the fossil record. In 2002, paleontologist Sankar Chatterjee (b. 1943) described a remarkable, though only partially complete, specimen of neognath bird from the Late Cretaceous of Antarctica. *Polarornis* is known from partial skull, vertebrae, pelvis, and limb elements. The beak was toothless, and the bird appears to be a member of the Gaviiformes, the modern loon family.

In 2005, a team led by paleontologist Julia Clarke described yet another important bird fossil from Antarctica. *Vegavis* was an extinct member of the Anseriformes, the modern bird group that is composed of ducks, geese, and other related waterfowl. The team conducted a detailed phylogenetic analysis of the traits of *Vegavis* and concluded that such extinct ancestors of modern birds did indeed live alongside the dinosaurs.

Both the Chatterjee and Clarke fossil birds push the existence of true Neornithes back to about 68 million or 70 million years ago, whereas molecular time estimates push the origin of modern birds back as far as 110 million years ago. This still leaves a considerable gap in the fossil record between what can be estimated in a computer and what has been found in the field. Understanding the origins of Neornithes certainly will improve in the near future, as molecular dates are more finely tuned and additional fossil evidence is forthcoming. For the time being, it appears that the disappearance of the dinosaurs probably provided an opportunity for the expansion of birds, but in considering this premise, one also must now accept growing evidence that some modern bird groups—particularly the Galliformes and Anseriformes—already had found some success earlier.

Neornithes Classification

Aves, consisting of all living and extinct groups of birds, is defined as all descendants of the most recent common ancestor of modern birds (*Passer domesticus*, the house sparrow, for example) and *Archaeopteryx*. The classification Neornithes, the modern birds, includes all living groups of birds and also represents the most recent common ancestor of all extant birds and that ancestor's descendants. Neornithes is further broken down into two major subgroups, the Paleognathae ("old jaws")—a group that includes about 55 extant species of flightless, often large birds—and the Neognathae ("new jaws"), a group that includes more than 9,000 species of many sizes and varieties.

The **phylogeny** of the Neornithes is a matter of continual study and debate. Generally speaking, modern birds share a remarkably wide set of traits despite their variability in other matters related to their **adaptations** to certain lifestyles. Modern birds lack the teeth and lengthy tails found in their dinosaurian ancestors but retain several traits from their Mesozoic roots, including the laying of amniotic eggs, clawed feet, and reptilelike scales on their legs and feet. Bird skulls are highly fused, lightweight, and have a toothless beak. All birds are feathered, a feature that first appeared in their non-avian dinosaurian ancestors as a means of insulation. All birds have skeletal features related to flight, even in those birds that have become secondarily flightless. Features of the flight skeleton include wings; lightweight, hollow limb bones; and large sections of fused vertebrae in the back to add strength and rigidity. These fundamental traits of birds have changed little during the past 50 million to 70 million years.

Despite their similarities, birds vary widely in their adaptations and **morphology** or shape. Along with fish, birds certainly are among the most successful vertebrates for having taken a basic body plan and developed highly specialized modifications to extend their reach to every corner of the globe.

The major groups and subgroups of neornithine birds are shown in the accompanying diagram. These groups are based

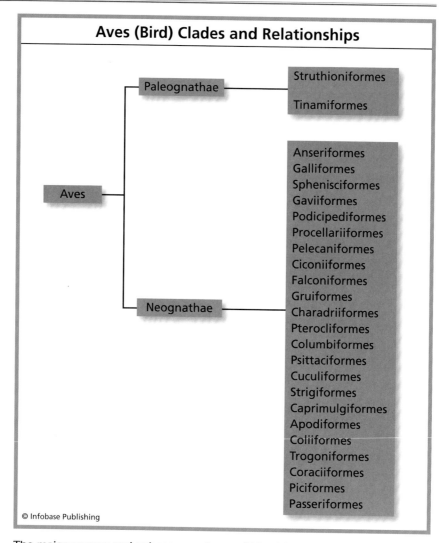

Aves (Bird) Clades and Relationships

Paleognathae
- Struthioniformes
- Tinamiformes

Aves

Neognathae
- Anseriformes
- Galliformes
- Sphenisciformes
- Gaviiformes
- Podicipediformes
- Procellariiformes
- Pelecaniformes
- Ciconiiformes
- Falconiformes
- Gruiformes
- Charadriiformes
- Pterocliformes
- Columbiformes
- Psittaciformes
- Cuculiformes
- Strigiformes
- Caprimulgiformes
- Apodiformes
- Coliiformes
- Trogoniformes
- Coraciiformes
- Piciformes
- Passeriformes

© Infobase Publishing

The major groups and subgroups of neornithine birds.

on two comprehensive modern studies of bird relationships, the *Handbook of the Birds of the World* (1992–2007) and *The Handbook of Australian, New Zealand and Antarctic Birds* (1990–2004).

Major Groups of Modern Birds

This section describes the general kinds of birds included in the order Neornithes, the families of all living modern birds, and provides some context for the discussion of extinct Cenozoic birds in the section that follows.

Paleognathae

This subgroup of modern birds includes two extant groups, the Struthioniformes and the Tinamiformes, as well as the extinct group Lithornithiformes. They are flightless birds and include many large members.

Struthioniformes. This group includes four subgroups and 10 living species, most notably the ostriches (Africa); emus and cassowaries (Australia and New Guinea); kiwis (New Zealand); and rheas (South America). The kiwi is the smallest living Struthioniforme, about the size of a chicken. The members of this group have powerful running legs; some species have only two toes.

Tinamiformes. This group includes a single group of about 45 species of small, flightless birds from South America. At about the size of a pigeon, the tinamous are the smallest living paleognaths.

Neognathae

This subgroup of modern birds includes 23 subgroups and more than 9,000 living species. The Neognathae are distinguished anatomically from the paleognaths by features of the palate (bones at the roof of the mouth) and ankles.

Anseriformes. This group includes three subgroups and about 150 species, found worldwide, of magpies, geese, swans, ducks, and screamers. The Anseriformes have webbed toes and broad bills.

Galliformes. This group includes eight subgroups and about 250 species, found worldwide except in northern Central Asia, of grouse, partridge, quail, turkeys, pheasants, guinea fowl, mound builders, chickens, and their close relatives. The Galliformes have rounded bodies and are not good flyers.

Sphenisciformes. This group includes about 16 species of penguins, all found in Antarctic and southern ocean waters. Penguins are flightless and have wings modified for swimming. They have thick coats of insulating feathers.

DINORNIS ELEPHANTOPUS.

The **Paleognathae**, or flightless birds, make up one of the two subgroups of Neornithes, the modern birds.

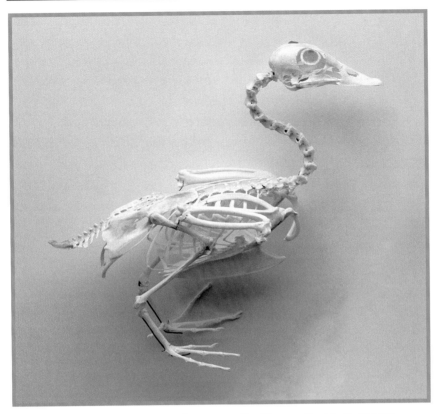

The subgroup of modern birds known as the **Neognathae** includes the majority of living birds, such as the crow pictured here.

Gaviiformes. This group includes five species from North America and Europe of loons and allied diving birds. These are aquatic birds with a spear-shaped bill.

Podicipediformes. This group includes 20 species, distributed worldwide, of grebes. These are freshwater diving birds with long necks and lobed toes.

Procellariiformes. This group includes four subgroups and 100 species, from trans-oceanic habitats, of albatross, petrels, diving petrels, storm petrels, and related species. The Procellariiformes are known for their tube-shaped bills and ability to traverse long stretches of ocean.

Pelecaniformes. This group includes six subgroups and about 50 species, distributed worldwide. Members include pelicans, gannets, cormorants, frigate birds, darters, tropicbirds, and related species. The Pelecaniformes are medium- to large-sized waterbirds with four webbed toes and, in many species, a distinctive throat pouch.

Ciconiiformes. This group includes seven subgroups and about 100 species, distributed worldwide, of herons, boatbills, storks, flamingos, shoebills, hammerkops, ibises and spoonbills, and related species. These birds are waders, with long legs and large bodies.

Falconiformes. This group includes five subgroups and about 260 species, distributed worldwide, of ospreys, hawks, eagles, buzzards, secretary birds, falcons, vultures, condors, and related species. These are carnivorous birds of prey, with keen vision, talons, and pointed beaks. They are mostly active during the day.

Gruiformes. This group includes nine subgroups and about 200 species, distributed worldwide, of cranes, limpkins, trumpeters, bustards, seriemas, sunbitterns, kagus, finfoots, coots, and their relatives. These are marsh birds with stiltlike legs.

Charadriiformes. This group includes 20 subgroups and about 300 species, distributed worldwide, of waders, shorebirds, snipes, jacanas, seed snipes, plains wanderers, gulls, terns, skimmers, plover, oystercatchers, avocets, ibis bills, sheathbills, Magellanic plover, thick-knees, button quail, auks, skuas, coursers, crab plover and related species. These are shorebirds with long legs and slender bills.

Pterocliformes. This group includes 16 species—found in Africa, Europe, and Asia—of sand grouse. These are small birds with pigeonlike heads and necks and long, pointed wings that live in semiarid and desert habitats.

Columbiformes. This group includes two subgroups and about 300 species, distributed worldwide, of pigeons, doves, and the extinct dodo. These birds have stout, round bodies and perching feet.

Psittaciformes. This group includes two subgroups and about 330 species, distributed to tropical and southern temperate zones, of cockatoos and parrots. These birds have well-developed vocal organs and strong, powerful beaks.

Cuculiformes. This group includes three subgroups and about 150 species, distributed worldwide, of turacos, roadrunners, cuckoos, hoatzins, and related species. These are shy birds with short wings, long tails, and a piercing cry.

Strigiformes. This group includes two subgroups and about 130 species, distributed worldwide, of owls and barn owls. These are nocturnal birds of prey with powerful beaks, good eyesight, and strong, clawed feet.

Caprimulgiformes. This group includes five subgroups and about 100 species, distributed worldwide, of nightjars, owlet-nightjars, potoos, frogmouths, oilbirds, and related species. These birds are insect eaters with a weak, gaping beak and an owl-like head.

Apodiformes. This group includes three subgroups and about 400 species, distributed worldwide, of swifts, tree swifts, humming-birds, and related species. The Apodiformes are rapid-flying birds with short legs, small bodies, and quickly flapping wings.

Coliiformes. This group includes a single subgroup and six species, found in sub-Saharan Africa, of moosebirds. These are small and slender birds with long, thin tails and hairlike body feathers.

Trogoniformes. This group includes a single subgroup and about 35 species—found in sub-Saharan Africa, the Americas, and Asia—of trogons and quetzals. The Trogoniformes are tropical birds with broad bills that live primarily in trees and do not fly great distances.

Coraciiformes. This group includes 12 subgroups and about 200 species, distributed worldwide, of kingfishers, todies, bee-eaters, rollers, hornbills, motmots, and related species. These birds have large heads, a large beak, and three forward-pointing toes.

Piciformes. This group includes six subgroups and about 400 species, distributed everywhere but Australasia, of jacamars, woodpeckers, toucans, honeyguides, barbets, puffbirds, and related species. These birds have chisel-like piercing beaks for penetrating wood and grasping feet.

Passeriformes. This group includes 91 subgroups and more than 5,000 species, distributed worldwide, of crows, robins, sparrows,

Some primitive bird groups did not survive until the Cenozoic Era. *Ichthyomis* was a member of a group of flying, toothed sea birds that have no living descendants.

mockingbirds, starlings, warblers, tyrant flycatchers, antbirds, wrens, larks, wagtails, thrushes, shrikes, finches, and related species. These are songbirds, with well-developed vocal organs, perching feet, and young that need to be cared for.

ANATOMY OF MODERN BIRDS

Modern birds share a number of **derived** characteristics, or **synapomorphies**, that distinguish them from their Mesozoic bird ancestors. Birds seem to have become completely "modernized" by the early Cenozoic, having discarded the teeth, long tails, clawed fingers, and other primitive, dinosaurian features that were still prominent in Mesozoic birds. Interestingly, the wings and feathers of modern birds—clearly their most distinguishing features—are not unique to modern birds and were shared by non-avian, maniraptoran dinosaurs and basal birds.

Bird anatomy and **physiology** are largely optimized for flight. The skeleton is lightweight, with hollow limb bones and hollow cavities for respiratory air sacs. Many of the bones that would be separate or jointed in other tetrapods are fused in birds for strength and economy of structure. The bones of the skull are tightly fused, and the orbit, or eye socket, is large. All modern birds have a toothless beak. The tail is reduced to only a few vertebrae, and in many species these bones are fused into a pygostyle, to which the tail feathers are attached.

The sternum, or breastbone, is large and keeled, for the attachment of flight muscles. The sternum is firmly joined to a fused segment of the spine by flat, segmented ribs. The hips and **sacral vertebrae** are fused into the synsacrum, strengthening the attachment of the legs. Each foot consists of three forward toes and one reversed toe, the hallux, which points backward and provides balance. Ankle bones and foot bones are largely fused.

The forelimbs are longer than the **hind limbs** and form the wings. The flight stroke in birds evolved from an earlier adaptation in small, feathered dinosaurs for reaching and grasping prey. The origin of bird flight is explored in another book in this series, *Last of the Dinosaurs*. Flightless birds also have wings, but the forelimbs may have been modified for other purposes, such as swimming (the penguin) or may remain underdeveloped in deference to another derived trait, such as larger body size and stronger legs for walking and running, such as the ostrich.

Features of the flight skeleton of birds include wings; lightweight, hollow limb bones; and large sections of fused vertebrae in the back to add strength and rigidity. These fundamental traits of birds have changed little during the past 50 million to 70 million years.

One of the most fascinating features of bird anatomy is the respiratory system. The lungs are small but are supplemented by four air sacs in the abdomen. The air sacs are connected to other parts of the skeleton through numerous air passages. When a bird inhales, most of the air passes through the lungs and flows directly to the air sacs. When a bird exhales, air returns from the air sacs to the lungs. Respiration—the absorption of oxygen by the lungs and tissues—takes place during both inhalation and exhalation. Essentially, a bird can breathe without stopping—unlike a mammal, which must pause to exhale air from its lungs before it can inhale again. The bird's respiratory system is the most efficient found

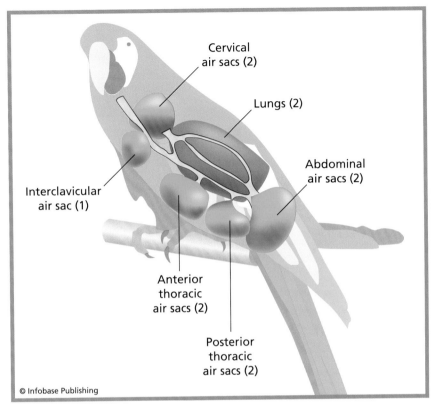

Because of a sophisticated respiratory system involving supplementary air sacs in the body cavity, respiration in birds takes place during both inhalation and exhalation. Essentially, a bird can inhale without pausing to exhale.

in terrestrial vertebrates. Birds inherited this complex respiratory system and the **pneumaticity** of their bones from their Saurischian dinosaur ancestors.

EXTINCT CENOZOIC BIRDS

The arc of climate change during the Cenozoic greatly affected the evolution of birds and other vertebrates. For the first 20 million years of the Cenozoic, from the Paleocene Epoch to the middle of the Eocene Epoch, the world was a subtropical place. Global warming peaked during the early Eocene, and tropical forests were present

(continues on page 54)

THINK ABOUT IT

From Reptiles to Birds: The Evolution of Bird Fingers

Fossils of Mesozoic reptiles, dinosaurs, and early birds clearly show transitional changes to skeletal structures that lead to birds. *Archaeopteryx* is a virtual mosaic of reptile and bird characteristics: These include the teeth and tail of a small dinosaur but the feathers and primitive wings of the first known bird.

The evolution of bird features is visible most clearly in the changing structure of the hand. The archosaurian stock from which the earliest dinosaurs arose had five fingers, like the crocodile. Beginning in the Late Triassic Epoch, with the earliest theropods such as *Herrerasaurus*, the fifth digit was greatly reduced to a mere, nonfunctional stub. *Coelophysis*, a somewhat later earlier theropod, had just four digits. By the time of *Allosaurus* (Late Jurassic, western North America), the hand had been reduced to three robust fingers. This also was the case for *Deinonychus* (Early Cretaceous, Montana), a maniraptoran dinosaur from the theropod line most closely associated with bird evolution. *Archaeopteryx*, the first bird, also had a three-fingered hand. Modern birds continued the trend in the modification of the hand. All modern birds have three fingers and also show a loss of the claws that once existed in their dinosaur ancestors.

In the study of the hand, paleontologists number the digits so that the presence of inherited traits can be linked from species to species in the evolutionary history of a clade. In the case of dinosaurs and birds, fossil evidence shows unambiguously that the digits of the bird wing are digits 1 through 3, the same digits as those of the theropod hand. As digits 1 through 3 were retained over time, digits 4 and 5 were lost. The middle finger, digit 2, is always the longest in the maniraptoran and bird hand, and it eventually became the primary structural support for the wing.

The study of vertebrate embryos can reveal traces of digits that once existed, in the form of cartilaginous fragments, in a group of embryonic animals but that do not ossify—become hardened bone—in the living animal once it is born. Bird embryos, for example, reveal the shadowy traces of two tiny stubs on the hand; these stubs disappear by the time the bird is born. Interestingly, the pattern of the digits seen in bird embryos appears to contradict the accepted ordering of digits in dinosaurs and birds. Rather than consisting of digits 1 through 3—the accepted order that appears to be so obvious through the study of fossil remains—the embryos of modern birds suggest that the lost digits are actually digits 1 and 5, and that the bird hand is made up of digits 2 through 4. If this were true, it would cast doubt on the evolutionary relationship of dinosaurs and birds.

It turns out that what is seen in bird embryos is not an accurate way of knowing which digits are which. In 2005, biologists Alexander O. Vargas and John F. Fallon published the results of studies of vertebrate embryos and the relationship of the embryonic state of the formative hand to the developmental state found in the organism after birth. It was once thought that digit identity—the size, shape, and arrangement of the digits—was programmed during the earliest embryonic state, even before cartilage cells began to develop a finger or toe. Vargas and Fallon demonstrated that digit identity is fixed much later in development and is not necessarily the same as the arrangement of the cartilaginous precursors of fingers and toes. In other words, the earliest traces of fingers seen in bird embryos, regardless of their arrangement, are unspecified until later in the process, as the formative digits interact with the biochemical programs of surrounding tissue. What may appear to be digits 2 through 4 in a chicken embryo will actually develop into digits 1 through 3. This research, rather than casting doubt on the dinosaur-bird link, actually lends more gravity to the theory.

(continued from page 51)

even at high latitudes. The great plains areas of the modern world were lush with tropical plants, rain forests, and warm, wet habitats. During that time, arboreal, or tree-dwelling, birds and mammals were dominant, and they browsed through dense forests. The ability to fly was not necessarily an advantage in such obstructed environments; this led to the appearance on the major continents of many large, flightless, predatory birds.

By about 45 million years ago, in the middle of the Eocene, global temperatures began to moderate after the breakup of Pangaea. Forests thinned out because of the worldwide cooling and drying effects of Antarctic glaciation. Grasses, whose origins reach back to the last days of the dinosaurs, began to spread widely during the Oligocene. An environment of patchy forests separated by large grassy plains and savannahs became the dominant habitat of the middle latitudes. This change in habitat spawned many lines of birds and mammals that were well adapted to living in wide-open spaces.

By about 6 million years ago, ice caps existed at both the North and South Poles, and the world was gripped by a periodic cycle of glaciation and ice ages. Today's world, which is considered to be in an interglacial span, includes a wide spectrum of habitats and climates, all of which have become home to a variety of birds and mammals. The accompanying chart illustrates the radiation of birds during the Cenozoic because of changes in climates and habitats.

Discussing the full catalog of extinct Cenozoic birds is beyond the scope of a single chapter in any book. The discussion below touches on some of the most interesting—and sometimes bizarre—ancestors of modern birds that have since vanished from the planet.

Extinct Flightless Birds (Paleognaths)

Flightless birds of the group Paleognathae include two living groups—the Struthioniformes, or ratites, and the Tinamiformes—as well as the extinct group Lithornithiformes. The tinamiformes are small, partridge-sized birds found in South and Central America. The ratites include the most familiar flightless birds: the ostriches (Africa); the cassowaries and emus (Australia); the rheas (South America); and the kiwis (New Zealand). The distribution of these modern flightless birds to continents of the Southern Hemisphere is a reminder of the effects of **geographic isolation** on the evolution of species.

The southern continents are the remaining pieces of Gondwana, the southern landmass that broke apart from Pangaea and separated into individual landmasses by the end of the Mesozoic Era. As a result of their isolation, Africa, South America, Australia, Madagascar, and New Zealand each has its own diverse evolutionary history. As Pangaea broke apart, Gondwana first became separated from the northern landmass known as **Laurasia**. It is presumed that the ancestors of modern ratites first arose during the Late Cretaceous Epoch, while Laurasia was still connected to Gondwana. As the continents and islands of the Southern Hemisphere drifted apart, the native ratites of each landmass evolved in slightly different ways and developed their own unique variations.

The shape of the sternum, or breastbone, of modern ratites suggests that their distant ancestors probably were fliers, and that their flightless condition evolved secondarily. Adaptation to a flightless lifestyle was especially prevalent in the Southern Hemisphere. On the islands of Madagascar and New Zealand, ratites acquired giant proportions; they sometimes measured 10 feet (3 m) tall. Such giant flightless birds were presumably predators and took advantage of a lack of large predatory mammals in their isolated island habitats. Such spectacular birds filled a niche not unlike that of their non-avian dinosaur ancestors.

Not all flightless birds are paleognaths. Penguins, rails, and the extinct great auk (Pleistocene, North America) and dodo (Pleistocene to recent, New Zealand and Micronesia) are examples of flightless birds of the group Neognathae. The development of gigantism in flightless birds also occurred elsewhere, in the form of several members of the Neognathes found in the Northern Hemisphere.

Several forms of giant, flightless predatory birds lived during the Cenozoic, including *Diatryma* (North America, shown here) and *Phorusrhacos* (South America).

Giant carnivorous birds such as *Diatryma* (Early Eocene, Europe and North America), discussed below, are an example of **convergent evolution**.

The fossil record of Paleognaths extends back at least to the Eocene Epoch and is represented by some remarkable giant specimens that lived from the Pleistocene to recent times, when the incursion of humans wiped many of these birds out.

Palaeotis (Middle Eocene, Germany) is one of the most primitive known ratite specimens and is represented only poorly, by several partial, crushed specimens. *Palaeotis* was a middle-sized flightless bird that measured about 4 feet (1.2 m) tall; it is possibly one of the earliest ostriches. The occurrence of ostrichlike fossils in the Eocene of Europe and the Miocene of Asia suggests that this type of ratite was widely distributed beyond Africa, the home of its extant descendants. *Palaeotis* was most likely a browsing **herbivore** that lived on fruits and seeds and other plant material. It had a stout body, slender legs, and a small head somewhat like that of a kiwi.

Dinornis (Pleistocene to recent, New Zealand), the giant moa, was the largest representative of the moa family, a group of flightless birds that lived on New Zealand. Of the 10 known moa species, *Dinornis* was the largest; it measured about 11 feet (3.3 m) tall. Although it was the tallest known bird that ever existed, *Dinornis* was relatively lightweight—about 550 pounds (250 kg)—when compared with the extinct *Aepyornis* (Pleistocene to recent, Madagascar), which weighed about twice as much. *Dinornis* had stout legs, a round body, and a long neck. Moas survived in New Zealand until about 1800; they fell victim to encroaching humans who burned their forest habitats to make room for farms and also hunted them into extinction. The emus of Australia are currently held to be relatives of the extinct moas.

The heaviest of all flightless birds was *Aepyornis* (Pleistocene to recent, Madagascar), which measured about 10 feet (3 m) tall and weighed more than 1,100 pounds (550 kg). Also known as the elephant bird, this taxon was native to Madagascar and coexisted with humans until it became extinct, by the 1600s. The reasons for the extinction of *Aepyornis* are a matter of debate. Despite the usual assumption that such large flightless birds were hunted to extinction by humans, recent archaeological studies of Madagascar native culture suggest that the birds were not hunted by humans. The birds' huge eggs—which measured up to 3.3 feet (1 m), the largest of any known vertebrate—may have been prized for food, however. Another study, headed by geologist Simon Clarke of the

University of Wollongong in Australia, looked at the chemical structure of the *Aepyornis* eggshell in relation to the known paleo-climate conditions of Madagascar during the past millennium. The Clarke-led study concluded that these great birds might have succumbed to changes in climate that affected the ability of their eggs to "breathe" properly.

Extinct Neognaths

Neognath birds share several common, derived features of the palate, ankle, and lower leg. In other respects, they are widely diverse and continue to confound the attempts of scientists to come to some agreement on the nature of their phylogeny. A spotty fossil record makes it doubly difficult to identify all of the critical ties that link extant birds to their ancestors. The descriptions below focus on several major groups of birds and their important extinct members and represent current thinking about which of these taxa belong in which groups.

Psittaciformes: Parrots

Psittacopes (Middle Eocene, Germany). Fossils of this basal member of the psittaciforms, or parrots, were found in lakebed sediments of Messel, Germany. The Messel shale beds are noteworthy for their extraordinary preservation of early mammals and birds that date from the Middle Eocene, about 49 million years ago—a time of rich faunal diversity that preceded a gradual deterioration of world climates and Cenozoic glaciation. The fossil record of early parrots is fragmentary and reaches back to the Early Eocene. *Psittacopes* is one of the best early parrot fossils and shows some of the characteristic features of these birds: the large head, short neck, and curved bill. In this taxon, the hooklike shape of the bill was not yet pronounced, however. *Psittacopes* was first described in 1998 from a specimen that was mostly complete except for the right leg; this added much to knowledge about the early development of parrots.

Piciformes: Woodpeckers and Toucans

Rupelramphastoides (Early Oligocene, Germany). The earliest members of the woodpeckers and toucans are difficult to trace in the fossil record. The Early Eocene bird *Neanis*, from the west-central United States, is known only from one poorly preserved but fairly complete specimen. *Rupelramphastoides* hails from a later time and is better preserved. It was described in 2005 by German paleontologist Gerald Mayr, a leading authority on Germany fossil birds. *Rupelramphastoides* represents one of the most complete specimens of an early member of this group. Although the skeletal remains were **disarticulated**, they make up a tiny, barbetlike bird that is also the smallest member of this group.

Apodiformes: Hummingbirds and Swifts

Eurotrochilus (Oligocene, Germany). Hummingbirds are the only group of birds in which most food gathering is done while hovering. To make this hovering possible, hummingbirds have a distinctively adapted sternum and wings. These traits, along with an elongated and narrow beak for sipping nectar from flowers, were present in the fossil *Eurotrochilus*, making it the oldest fossil that resembles modern hummingbirds. Hummingbirds are one of several kinds of birds that pollinate flowers. Flowers can coevolve with their pollinating agents over time: Both a flower and its pollinator can develop mutually beneficial biological modifications. *Eurotrochilus* represents the earliest specimen of hummingbird discovered in Europe and pushes back to the early Oligocene the estimated time of the **coevolution** of birds and flowers.

Pelecaniformes: Pelicans and Cormorants

Limnofregata (Early Eocene, Wyoming). Frigate birds are specialized marine birds, related to pelicans, that spend most of their life airborne over the water. Frigate birds are predators, and they feed primarily on fish. Frigate birds spend time on land only during breeding season. *Limnofregata* ("freshwater frigate bird") was an early form of frigate bird with an average wingspan of about 3.3 feet (1 m). Discovery of seven new specimens in 2005, including a new species of *Limnofregata*, showed that some individuals were about 20 percent larger than the average. Some of these fossil specimens had well-preserved impressions of feathers. The characteristically narrow, pointed, and slightly downturned beak of these birds was evident in these early members of the taxon. One distinct difference between *Limnofregata* and modern frigate birds is the size and shape of the foot. Extant frigate birds have small feet and reduced webbing, whereas *Limnofregata* has long toes and extensive webbing; this would have made it more at home while paddling in the water.

Osteodontornis (Late Miocene, California). This waterbird had a suite of features reminiscent of pelicans and albatrosses. It was a large, heavily built bird with a wingspan up to 20 feet (6 m) and a body length of 4 feet (1.2 m); it was the second-largest flying bird ever, after *Argentavis*. *Osteodontornis* ("Orr's bony-toothed bird") is so-named because its bill was lined with false teeth composed of small, pointed outgrowths of bone. The roof of the mouth—the palate—was deeply grooved so that the bony teeth of the lower jaw could be inset when the mouth was closed. *Osteodontornis* had long and narrow wings and may have needed to leap from high cliffs to send its large body into flight. It had a strongly S-curved and heavy bill that it probably held between its shoulders like modern pelicans. To feed, *Osteodontornis* swept down over the water to snag fish and squid on the bony teeth of its bill. As with its modern descendants, *Osteodontornis* probably had a throat pouch for storing its catch of the day.

Copepteryx (Late Oligocene to Early Miocene, Japan). *Copepteryx* was part of an extinct family of pelecaniforms known as Plotopteridae; it was a family of flightless, penguinlike diving birds. Unrelated to true penguins, the plotopterids are example of convergent evolution, having developed a wing-propelled method of diving similar to that of penguins. One specimen of *Copepteryx* consists only of a giant **femur**—a hind limb bone—but represents the largest known diving bird, living or fossil.

Gruiformes: Cranes and Marsh Birds

Neocathartes (Late Eocene to Early Miocene, Wyoming). This carnivorous ground bird had long, strong legs and may have spent more time chasing prey on the ground than in flight. *Neocathartes* ("walking new turkey vulture") was not a true vulture but a member of the cranes and marsh birds. *Neocathartes* is sometimes likened to the modern secretary bird, which grasps or holds down prey with its sharply clawed feet while it pecks away with its hawklike beak. *Neocathartes* was moderately large; it was about 18 inches (46 cm) long, with a wingspan of about 3 feet (1 m).

Pumiliornis (Middle Eocene, Germany). The Gruiformes (cranes) and Charadriiformes (snipes and waders) together include more than 500 species of modern shorebirds. *Pumiliornis* is something of an evolutionary intermediate between these two groups, but with a foot that is more like that of a dove (columbiform)—a bird that is far from being a shorebird. *Pumiliornis* truly includes a mosaic of traits found in several modern bird taxa without clearly belonging to any. Its exquisitely preserved skeleton shows a bird that was about 12 inches (30 cm) long from the tip of its long, narrow, downward-sloping bill to the tips of its toes. The neck was medium length, with an S-curve shape. The toes were short and clawed, and *Pumiliornis* differed from all known shorebirds by having a perching foot.

Palaelodus (Early to Middle Oligocene, France). This small wading bird was a distant ancestor of the flamingo. Although several specimens of *Palaelodus* have been found, little is known of the bird's skull. The shape and size of its feet, with long toes, suggest that it was more comfortable wading in the water and dipping its head to catch fish than it was diving or swimming. It stood about 24 inches (61 cm) tall.

Phorusrhacos (Early to Middle Miocene, Argentina). Among the ancestors of the cranes and marsh birds is an unexpected surprise in the fossil record: a large, flightless, predatory bird that once roamed South America attacking small mammals such as primitive horses. The presence of *Phorusrhacos* and other, similar, flightless predatory birds in South America filled an ecological niche left vacant by the disappearance of the theropod dinosaurs. The evolution of unrelated flightless predatory birds on several continents and at different times is an example of convergent evolution. *Phorusrhacos* stood about 7.8 feet tall (2.4 m) and had strong running legs. Its wings were reduced to vestigial appendages and probably were too short to play an active role in capturing prey, even though, in some cases, each forelimb was capped with a robust, spikelike claw. The skull was large, with a high, bony beak capable of crushing bone.

Phorusrhacos is a member of a larger family of Phorusrhacidae—known as the terror birds—that originated in South America and included at least one North American taxon, *Titanis*. *Titanis* found its way north as a result of the land bridge established between the Americas. In South America, eight fossil Phorusrhacidae taxa are known from the Early Miocene to Early Pliocene. The birds ranged in size from about 31 inches (80 cm) to 9 feet (2.75 m). The largest phorusrhacid was *Brontornis*, which had a body mass of about 900 pounds (400 kg). A recently discovered skull of a large and as-yet-unnamed phorusrhacid measured about 2.4 feet (72 cm) long—the largest known of all avian skulls.

Anseriformes and Galliformes: Ducks and Game Fowl

The Anseriformes and Galliformes make up a group of related waterfowl and game birds called the Galloanseri. These birds represent the earliest and most basal Neognathes, the largest group of living birds.

Diatryma (Early Eocene, Europe, North America). The giant, flightless *Diatryma* ("canoe," for the shape of its large skull) is as unlike a duck as it can be and still be called a bird. This bird is yet another example of convergent evolution, as some Paleogene birds adapted a flightless, terrestrial predatory lifestyle. Closely related to its European cousin *Gastornis*—some say they are one and the same animal—*Diatryma* was about 7 feet (2.1 m) tall; walked on muscular legs with large, clawed feet; and had a large head with an oversized, sharp beak. Although it has been suggested that *Diatryma* was herbivorous and that its bony beak was perhaps best suited for crushing seeds, it appears to have all of the weapons, and the size, to be the dominant predator in its North American landscape. *Diatryma* is often depicted in illustrations grabbing smaller grazing animals, such as early horses, with its deadly beak and devouring them.

Presbyornis (Late Paleocene to Early Eocene, Europe, North America, and South America). A more ducklike member of the Anseriforms is *Presbyornis*, known from many good specimens from Wyoming and other locations. *Presbyornis* is one of the earliest known anseriforms but already shows the characteristic traits of the group. It was a long-legged and long-necked swimmer and wader about the size of a goose or swan. *Presbyornis* had a broad and flat bill and is presumed to have filtered small food items from the water in the manner of modern ducks. The anatomy of *Presbyornis*, with its long legs and neck but ducklike bill and paddling feet, could be viewed as a mosaic of ducks and flamingos. Some specimens have been found in extensive groups, suggesting that *Presbyornis* lived in colonies.

Passeriformes: Songbirds

Songbirds are the largest extant bird group, with more than 5,000 living species—more than half of all living birds. Paleontological and accumulating biochemical and molecular evidence point to a Gondwanan origin of songbirds. The earliest passerine fossils are fragmentary remains of wrens from Australia that date from the Early Eocene. The earliest fossil record of songbirds in the Northern Hemisphere dates to the Early Oligocene. Molecular time estimates developed by Swedish biologist Per Ericson and his colleagues in 2002 suggest that wrens seen in New Zealand today are remnants of the earliest appearance of songbirds, and that their origins probably extend back to the Late Cretaceous Epoch, between 82 million and 85 million years ago.

Modern orders of passerine birds were well established by the Oligocene Epoch. Most extinct passerine species superficially resembled their living descendants.

Unnamed Acanthisitidae (Early Eocene, Australia). The earliest known songbirds are basal wrens from Australia whose fragmentary remains consist only of limb elements. Their appearance predated that of songbirds in the Northern Hemisphere by about 25 million years.

Wieslochia (Early Oligocene, Germany). The earliest songbird fossil from Europe is that of *Wieslochia*, a small passerine about the size of a house sparrow. It is known from two specimens, one consisting of a disarticulated skeleton and the other a cranium with mandible.

Sphenisciformes: Penguins

Waimanu (Late Paleocene, New Zealand). Penguin fossils are among the oldest preserved remains of neornithine birds. Excellent remains of four partial individuals of *Waimanu* show that penguins had already diverged from other birds in developing a stout, upright posture, large body size, and wing-propelled diving ability by the earliest part of the Cenozoic Era. *Waimanu* was about the size of the extant emperor penguins, the males of which stand up to 3.6 feet (1.1 m) tall and weigh about 17 pounds (37 kg).

Charadriiformes: the Auks

Pinguinus (Pleistocene to recent, Europe, Greenland, Iceland, and North America). The recently extinct *Pinguinus,* or great auk, was a moderately large, flightless bird whose wings were modified for swimming and diving. *Pinguinus* was not directly related to modern penguins, which live only in the Southern Hemisphere. Auks lived in the Northern Hemisphere but were similarly adapted. *Pinguinus* thus was an example of convergent evolution. *Pinguinus* had the general body plan of a penguin, but with feet set further back on the body and a tall, deep bill. *Pinguinus* also resembled the penguin in lifestyle: It lived in colonies, dove into the water to catch fish, and was able only to waddle slowly while walking on land. *Pinguinus* was hunted into extinction by 1844; the last of the *Pinguinus* lived near Iceland. Modern auks, including puffins and auklets, live in northern waters and are capable of flying.

Coliiformes (Moosebirds)

Oligocolius (Oligocene, Germany). Coliiformes is a small group of tiny, slender birds from sub-Saharan Africa known as short fliers and excellent runners while on the ground. *Oligocolius*, described in 2000, is the earliest known moosebird and is based on a well-preserved but disarticulated specimen from the rich marine deposits of Frauenweiler, Germany—a site normally known for fossils of fish and diving birds. *Oligocolius* represents one of the few land birds found in this once near-shore environment; this suggests that it died in midair and tumbled down into the water over which it was flying. *Oligocolius* differs from modern moosebirds in the proportions of its wing bones; these proportions made this extinct taxon better at sustained flight than modern moosebirds. The feet of *Oligocolius* were better suited for climbing than for running, so it is likely that *Oligocolius* was less able to move quickly along the ground than extant members of this taxon.

Columbiformes: Pigeons and Doves

Raphus (Pleistocene to recent, Mauritius). Commonly known as the dodo, this large, bulky ancestor of pigeons evolved on the southern island of Mauritius, which was relatively free of large predators. The bird stood about 3.3 feet (1 m) tall, was flightless, and had a round body with a tuftlike tail. *Raphus* was forest dwelling and lived on ripe fruit, which it probed and divided using the downturned point of its 9-inch (23 cm) bill and snout. *Raphus* also may have waded into water to catch fish. Early illustrations of dodos showed them as fat, lazy animals, but this was probably a result of overfeeding in captivity. More recent research and illustrations have trimmed a few pounds from *Raphus*, but it was a large bird, nonetheless; *Raphus* weighed as much as 50 pounds (23 kg).

Dodos became extinct during the seventeenth century because of the arrival on Mauritius of humans, who ripped apart the bird's forest habitat, hunted it, and brought dogs and cats that may have done the same. There also is evidence that a natural disaster on Mauritius about 500 years ago may have wiped out a large number of the birds long before the arrival of Europeans. Current knowledge about the dodo was greatly improved in 2005, when a team of Dutch and Mauritian scientists discovered a fossil bone bed consisting of several individual dodos of various sizes, from juvenile to adult. The same team found a more complete individual skeleton in 2006.

Falconiformes: Falcons, Eagles, and Vultures

There is some debate over the classification and relationships among taxa included in the Falconiformes. One view groups the New World vultures and condors with the storks, or Ciconiiformes. For the purposes of this book, a widely accepted view of Falconiformes defines the group as including the New World vultures, condors, ospreys, hawks, eagles, secretary birds, falcons, and caracaras.

Argentavis (Late Miocene, Argentina). This extinct giant vulture is the largest known flying bird. With an enormous wingspan of 28 feet (8.3 m) and a body length of about 12 feet (3.5 m), the head height of *Argentavis* was about that of a 6-foot (1.8 m) human. *Argentavis* was twice as big as the largest living flying bird, the albatross. This predatory bird had strong legs and large, clawed feet. It probably flew by gliding on thermal currents and intermittently flapping its wings—a strategy to conserve energy that is seen in large extant birds. Like its living relatives, the vultures, *Argentavis* probably was a carrion eater, although it also may have attacked prey such as marsupial mammals if it could pounce easily on them from above.

Teratornis (Early to Late Pleistocene, North America). *Teratornis* was one of the largest prehistoric birds of North America. Known primarily from more than 100 specimens from the western United States, this early condor had a wingspan of up to 12 feet (3.8 m). It had a somewhat larger bill than a modern condor, suggesting that *Teratornis* may have been more active as a predator than the condor, which is primarily a scavenger. Many specimens of *Teratornis* have been recovered from the Rancho La Brea tar pits in Los Angeles. This shows that these predatory birds probably were attracted by the plight of mammals and other creatures stuck in the liquid asphalt and then got trapped themselves to be dragged down to their death. The legs of *Teratornis* were relatively weak and not suited to running along the ground; this suggests that this bird probably flapped its wings vigorously in order to lift its great weight to take off. The bones of the pelvic region and hind limbs suggest that *Teratornis* was an able walker, even if not a runner, and was best suited to stalking, rather than running, while on the ground.

A diversity of extinct mammal and bird fossils have been found at the Rancho La Brea tar pits near Los Angeles.

Harpagornis (Pleistocene to recent, New Zealand). This early eagle from New Zealand was the largest of all known eagles but was not as enormous as its vulture and condor cousins. With its 10-foot (3 m) wingspan, this able bird of prey probably was a natural enemy of the slower and vulnerable moas and certainly was a top predator of Pleistocene New Zealand. Evidence for this predator-prey relationship exists in the form of claw marks found on fossil remains of moas. *Harpagornis* had the sharply hooked bill and talons characteristic of modern eagles. Its powerful legs would have allowed

Harpagornis to spring into the air, and it probably swooped down from high perches to attack such prey as moas and flightless geese.

THE AGE OF BIRDS

Although the Cenozoic Era usually is dubbed the Age of Mammals, it also is rightfully the Age of Birds. It was during the current era that modern bird families established their dominance of the air, diversified into more than 9,000 species, and radiated to all parts of the world. In some parts of the world, birds took over where their dinosaur ancestors left off, becoming the dominant predators in their habitats, particularly in the island worlds of the Southern Hemisphere.

The fossil record of the first bird raises many questions about the very definition of a bird. Before the recent discovery of small, feathered, non-avian theropod dinosaurs, it was believed that any vertebrate with true feathers was a bird. Other characteristics once believed to be unique to birds now have also been found in dinosaurs. These characteristics include a respiratory system using air sacs, a bony beak, probable warm-bloodedness, and gizzards and stomach stones. Even powered flight is not unique to birds, having evolved separately on two other occasions in other vertebrates.

What makes birds evolutionarily unique is the combination of these features and the development of a basic body plan that includes feathers, wings, a tail, a bipedal stance, clawed feet, a largely fused backbone, a toothless beak, and strong sensory organs that have been further adapted by all sizes and kinds of birds to enable them to live almost anywhere on any continent. Birds are at once the most specialized vertebrates and the most similar among themselves. It is no wonder that there is no confusing a bird with any other known kind of creature.

SUMMARY

This chapter explored the remarkable success of birds during the Cenozoic and described some of the most remarkable extinct members of the taxon.

1. The first birds evolved from small, flightless theropod dinosaurs during the Middle and Late Jurassic Epochs. *Archaeopteryx* (Late Jurassic, Germany) represents the first true bird that is known from the fossil record.

2. Most of these modern bird groups arose during the Cenozoic Era, after the K-T extinction of the dinosaurs and pterosaurs. Bird anatomy had become completely "modernized" by the early Cenozoic, having discarded the teeth, long tails, clawed fingers, and other primitive dinosaurian features that were still prominent in Mesozoic birds.

3. Modern birds are classified as Neornithes ("new birds") and are divided into two subgroups, the Paleognathae, or flightless birds, and the Neognathae, the huge group that includes the majority of living birds.

4. Research using molecular time estimation and some recent fossil discoveries has shed new light on origins of modern birds; scientists now conclude that some lines of Neornithes did indeed have roots in the Cretaceous.

5. Among the Neornithes, the group Paleognathae ("old jaws") includes about 55 extant species of flightless, often large, birds. The Neognathae ("new jaws") include more than 9,000 species of many sizes and varieties of the most familiar birds, including waterbirds, game fowl, songbirds, and birds of prey.

6. The evolutionary relationships among groups of modern birds are a matter of continual study and debate. There are about 25 recognized major groups or families of living birds.

7. The bird body is lightweight and optimized for flight. The bird respiratory system is the most efficient found in terrestrial vertebrates and allows a bird to breathe continuously, unlike mammals, which must pause to exhale air from their lungs before they can inhale again.

8. Convergent evolution and the isolation of fauna on continents and islands resulted in the emergence of large, flightless birds

at different times throughout the Cenozoic Era. Some of these large birds became the dominant predators of their habitats.

9. The largest known flying bird was *Argentavis* (Late Miocene, Argentina), with a wingspan of 28 feet (8.3 m).

SECTION THREE:
EVOLUTION OF
THE MAMMALS

3

EARLY MAMMALS

The ascendancy of mammals as the most dominant vertebrates of the Cenozoic Era is rooted in the same evolutionary stock that gave rise to reptiles (lizards, crocodiles, and dinosaurs) and to birds. By the Late Carboniferous Period, about 310 million years ago, reptiles became the first vertebrates to break away from a life bound to the water. This accomplishment was the result of a new reproductive adaptation, the amniotic egg. **Amniotes** produce eggs with a protective outer membrane; this adaptation made it possible for the animals to breed out of the water. Modern amniotes include reptiles, mammals, and birds. The story of the first amniotes is told in another book in this series, *March Onto Land*.

By the beginning of the Permian Period, about 299 million years ago, basal amniotes had begun to branch into four distinct clades. The distinguishing features of these four groups were many, but they began with a simple distinction in the design of the animals' skulls: the presence and location of **temporal fenestrae**. These are openings, or "windows" (*fenestra* is the Latin word for *window*), in the skull; they are located just behind the orbits on the sides of the skull, or temple region. The windows in the skull added lightness without compromising strength and also provided additional edges and crannies to which stronger and more complex jaw muscles could be attached. Each of the four groups of amniotes developed variations on skull anatomy that best suited their survivability and adaptation to the world in which they lived. From these four groups of amniotes arose all of the terrestrial vertebrate families known today.

By the start of the Middle Triassic Epoch, 245 million years ago, four evolutionary lines of reptiles had become well established.

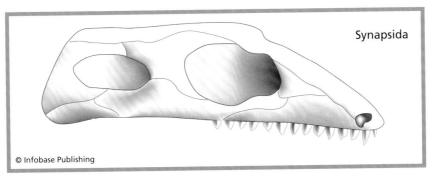

Synapsida

© Infobase Publishing

Synapsid skull

These were the **Anapsida** (basal amniotes); the **Synapsida** (mammals and their ancestors); the **Diapsida** (lizards, snakes, crocodiles, dinosaurs, birds, and pterosaurs); and the **Euryapsida** (marine reptiles).

The roots of all of today's mammals are found in the evolution of the synapsids. The first mammals arose during the Late Triassic Epoch and slowly diversified throughout the Mesozoic Era. As the natural history of the Mesozoic Era unfolded, the evolution and radiation of mammals was held in check by the success of the larger and more dominating dinosaurs and pterosaurs. It was not until after the K-T mass extinction removed dinosaurs from the picture 65.5 million years ago that mammals had an opportunity to diversify more rapidly and widely and to become dominant in their own right. This chapter explains the traits that form the basis of modern mammal anatomy and traces the history of early mammals during the Mesozoic.

EVOLUTION OF MAMMAL BIOLOGY

The reptile group known as the Synapsida included the ancestral mammals. True mammals did not appear until the Late Triassic Epoch, but evolutionary developments leading to true mammals began as far back as the Early Permian.

Synapsids included two groups of animals. The pelycosaurs were large, sailbacked animals that lived from the Late Carboniferous to the Late Permian Periods. They were joined by a mixed group of predatory and herbivorous synapsids collectively known as **Therapsida** and more commonly referred to as the **mammal-like reptiles**.

Pelycosaurs such as the large-bodied *Dimetrodon* (Late Permian, North America and Europe) and *Edaphosaurus* (Late Carboniferous to Early Permian, Texas) probably were "cold-blooded," or **ectothermic**. They may have used their sail backs to warm themselves in the sun. They walked very much like a crocodile, with a sprawling gait and a belly barely off the ground. *Dimetrodon* was one of the largest predators of its time. *Edaphosaurus* was an herbivore, one of the earliest on record. Its shallow jaws were lined on the perimeter with uniformly sized chisel-like teeth that the animal used to snip vegetation.

The Evolution of Mammal-like Traits

The therapsids arose during the Middle Permian, following the decline of the pelycosaurs. Anatomically, therapsids marked a change in body plan from the sprawling pelycosaurs. The therapsid body was more compact, the tail was reduced, and the legs were longer. These changes made therapsids better walkers than the belly-dragging pelycosaurs. The reduction of tail length reduced the surface area of the skin, thereby easing the loss of body heat and allowing these animals to maintain a steadier body temperature. These adaptations were leading to **endothermy,** or "warm-bloodedness," a significant innovation exploited by true mammals.

Three important groups of therapsids were the dinoceplalids, the dicynodonts, and the cynodonts. The dinocephalids, or "terrible heads," were a group of carnivorous and herbivorous therapsids with deep, large skulls and stocky bodies. All of the dinocephalids became extinct at the Permian-Triassic boundary.

The dicynodonts, or "two dog teeth," were a geographically widespread group of herbivores that ranged in size from that of a small rodent to more than 10 feet (3 m) long. With the exception of a few taxa, most dicynodonts also were wiped out by the end-Permian mass extinction.

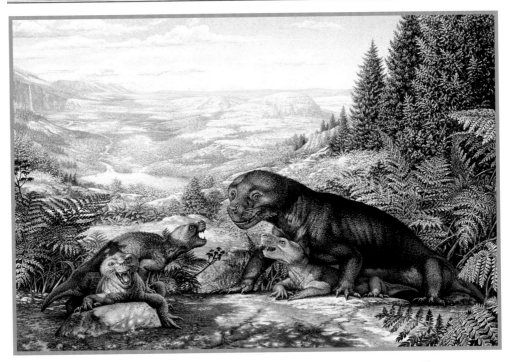

The most likely ancestors of mammals were a group of reptiles known as the cynodonts. *Thrinaxodon* is pictured here with its pups.

The most critical link between therapsids and true mammals was represented by the cynodonts, the mammal-like reptiles whose name means "dog teeth." These small, predatory synapsids grew increasingly plentiful and specialized during the Triassic Period and were most likely the ancestors of mammals. The evolutionary transformation of synapsid reptiles to mammals is one of the clearest cases of transitional modifications in the fossil record of vertebrates.

Even early cynodonts such as the long-nosed *Procynosuchus* (Later Permian, southern Africa) had affinities with true mammals. Among other anatomical features, attributes such as an enlarged nasal passage; a small, but increasingly more complex, mosaic of jaw muscles, teeth, and bone; and a more flexible joint connecting the neck and the spine gave this small animal a look reminiscent of a modern rodent. While the overall appearance of *Procynosuchus* was strikingly mammal-like, the story of the transition from reptiles to mammals is told most clearly through an examination of stages in the development of the jaw mechanics of the cynodonts.

During the early evolution of the synapsids, the lower jaw was made up of many different bones. Over time, especially in the cynodonts, some of these individual jaw bones either diminished in size or were displaced entirely by one larger bone called the **dentary**. Other stages in this transformation of the jaws included the development of several equally strong muscle groups for the jaw and the consolidation of bones in the back of the skull; these developments provided strength to the bite and chewing ability of these animals. Most reptiles can move their jaws only up and down. In contrast, mammals can chew using a triangulation pattern—a key adaptation for the development of more complex tooth batteries that can be used to chew meat or a wide variety of vegetation. Stages in the development of transformation of the jaws first took place in the evolution of the cynodont herbivores.

Another gradual but radical anatomical change to cynodont jaws resulted in the development of mammal-like hearing in cynodonts. In other synapsids, such as *Dimetrodon*, the lower jaw consisted of numerous small bones at the rear of the skull that formed the jaw joint. The eardrum was behind the jaw. In the cynodont *Thrinaxodon*, a change can be seen in the arrangement of these smaller jaw bones. As the dentary bone became larger, and some of the small bones at the back of the lower jaw formed a new type of jaw joint, several of the remaining bones became smaller and migrated toward the ear region. In the earliest mammals, the same small bones were present but no longer were associated with the jaw joint. Instead, these bones had been adapted as the anatomical base of the hearing mechanism, and thus changed their function.

Thermoregulation, the control of body temperature, was an additional challenge for land animals. Tetrapods must attain a certain optimum internal body temperature before they can become fully active for walking, feeding, hunting, and other physical activity. Large synapsids such as the pelycosaurs and dicynodonts relied on their large body size to slow the gain or loss of heat, but their size also made them relatively slow moving. Smaller animals, such as the cynodonts, did not have this size advantage. Instead, cynodonts probably maintained their body heat by eating frequently and remaining physically active to burn calories, and by doing so developed the endothermic thermoregulatory scheme seen in true mammals.

As explained below, the benefits of endothermy are clear. The cost of evolving a warm-blooded physiology was great, however, because such a physiology requires a tenfold increase in the consumption of food energy. Paleontologist David B. Norman suggests that the improved jaw designs of cynodonts played an important role in making it possible for the cynodonts to develop early endothermy. Improvements to the cynodonts' ability to chew enabled the food they consumed to be digested more rapidly. A gradual separation of the nasal passages from the mouth cavity in cynodonts also allowed the animals to breathe and chew at the same time, a need most evident only in warm-blooded creatures.

Cynodonts were small; most were no longer than 2 feet (61 cm) long. The Early Triassic taxon *Thrinaxodon* (South Africa and Antarctica) was about 17 inches (45 cm) long, including its catlike tail, and clearly showed changes in the posture and gait of cynodont reptiles.

Cynognathus (Middle Triassic, South Africa, Antarctica, and China) was a doglike carnivore and one of the largest of the cynodonts, at about 3.5 feet (1 m) long. Undoubtedly, *Cynognathus* was a fierce predator; it also represented another important milestone in the evolution of true mammals. *Cynognathus* had long canine teeth for stabbing prey; small, pointed incisors for gripping prey; and serrated cheek teeth for shredding the flesh of its victims. The dentary bone of *Cynognathus* provides evidence of the consolidation of the lower jaw bones that led to a stronger bite.

An even more doglike cynodont was *Probelesodon* (Late Triassic, Argentina). Its limbs were more fully erect than those of earlier cynodonts, and this improved posture gave this dog-sized predator speed and maneuverability.

Anatomical modifications in cynodonts such as *Thrinaxodon*, *Cynognathus*, and *Probelesodon* led to innovations in posture, skull and jaw mechanics, sensory functions, thermoregulation, and locomotion that in turn led to the establishment of a suite of traits that are all culminated in a new species of vertebrate, the characters of true mammals.

Traits of True Mammals

The textbook definition of a mammal is a vertebrate that has hair and produces milk to nurse its young.

Mammary glands, present in females, secrete milk that mothers use to nourish their newborn young. All mammals—even those, such as whales, that live in the ocean—produce milk for this purpose. Milk is a highly nutritious liquid that contains a rich mixture of proteins, sugar, and fat. Mammary glands are naturally linked to the special amniotic reproduction strategy of mammals, in which the unborn embryo incubates inside the mother's body. The word *mammal* itself is derived from the Latin term for mammary gland.

Hair is unique to mammals and comes in many forms, from the sparse bristles found on whales and dolphins to the thick fur of many terrestrial mammals. Hair is composed largely of dead cells filled with the protein keratin. Individual hairs are rooted in the skin by a tiny, bulblike follicle beneath the skin surface. The evolution of fur is linked to thermoregulation: Fur provides insulation from excessive heat loss. The hooves and horns present in some mammals also are composed of keratin. Some horns, such as those of cattle and antelope, have a bony core that is wrapped in a sheath of keratin.

Many stages of evolution took place between the emergence of basal amniotes, in the Early Permian Period and the emergence of the first mammals, in the Late Triassic Epoch—a span of some 45 million years. The fossil record of mammalian ancestors shows a relatively gradual sequence of trait loss and acquisition that resulted in the specialized features that culminated in a formula for lasting success and in mammals' persistent adaptability to environmental changes. Evolutionary biologist Thomas S. Kemp of Oxford University divides the traits shared by all mammals into five categories: adaptations to the jaw and teeth; modifications to limb and posture affecting locomotion; brain size and sensory organs; endothermic temperature regulation; and the emergence of particular bioregulatory systems such as the kidneys. The antecedents of mammals had some, but not all, of these traits. The important features of these signature mammal traits are discussed below.

Mammal Jaws and Teeth

Mammal skulls differ significantly from those of reptiles. The key differences are related to articulation of the jaw and the nature of mammalian teeth.

Reptile jaws articulate using two small bones at the back of the jaw. In mammals, those small bones found in reptilian ancestors have become the bones of the middle ear. The mammal jaw is hinged by a single bone of the lower jaw, or dentary. Only the lower jaw of the mammal can move to open and close the mouth.

In most reptiles, the teeth are **homodont**, or similarly cone-shaped. There is little difference, except in size, between reptile teeth in the front, middle, and back of the jaw. Reptiles also replace their teeth whenever they lose them, throughout life. Not only do mammals have **heterodont** dentition—different types of teeth for different purposes—but most mammals also have only two sets of teeth during their lifetime.

There are some exceptions to heterodonty in mammals; one such example is the dolphin, whose teeth are uniformly conical. There also are some mammalian taxa whose teeth have been highly modified to the extent that they no longer resemble familiar mammalian teeth. Examples of such modifications can be seen in the greatly reduced teeth of anteaters and in the loss of teeth altogether in baleen whales.

Another difference between reptiles' and mammals' teeth is the way that the dentition is attached to the jaw. In reptiles, teeth are attached to the top edge or inside ridge of the bony jaw. The teeth of mammals have roots that are set into sockets in the jaw.

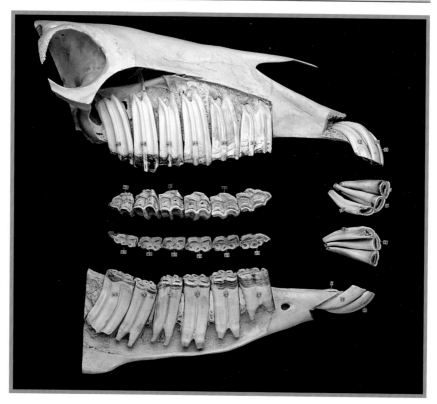

The teeth of mammals, such as the horse, have roots that are set into sockets in the jaw.

The adult mammal may have four basic kinds of teeth:

Incisors. These are chisel-like, in the front of the mouth, and used for nipping, gnawing, and grasping. These are single-rooted teeth.

Canines. These are long, conical teeth on either side of the incisors; the canines are used for grasping, killing, and tearing prey. Canines also are single-rooted.

Premolars. Located next to the canines, premolars are broader, flatter teeth with one or two roots. They are used for chewing.

Molars. These are the broadest chewing teeth and are located in the back of the mouth. Upper molars have two roots, and lower molars have three roots.

Mammal teeth provide excellent clues to the lifestyle of a given taxon. Teeth and jaws reveal much about a mammal's feeding habits. Large canine teeth usually indicate a predatory lifestyle, whereas a preponderance of incisors and molars indicates an animal that might snip away at plants and grind them to a pulp inside the mouth. Some mammals, such as humans, have a suite of teeth suited to both carnivory and omnivory.

The number and positioning of each kind of tooth is highly variable by mammal taxon. So distinctive are the tooth designs and patterns of mammals' teeth that many fossil mammal species are named on the basis of preserved teeth alone. Paleontologists and zoologists use a **dental formula** to describe the kind and number of teeth in one-half of the upper and lower jaw as a means to identify given mammal taxa. The scientists use a grid to number different kinds of teeth found in the jaw. The distinctive tooth patterns of fossil mammals provide excellent clues to the evolutionary ties that link different mammalian groups. The science of mammalian teeth is so refined that a single fossil tooth often can be associated with a given kind of mammal based on the number, shape, size, and position of the tooth's cusps—the points on a canine tooth or molar.

The best clues to the lifestyle of an extinct mammal are found in its teeth. Fortunately, the hard, enameled composition of teeth makes them one of the most likely parts of an animal to become fossilized. The distinguished Finnish paleontologist Björn Kurtén (1924–1988) wrote eloquently about the eating habits revealed by fossil mammal teeth. High-crowned cheek teeth indicated grass eaters, such as horses or bison, whose teeth wore down to an efficient grinding surface. Browsing woodland herbivores, such as deer and ancient giraffes, had lower tooth crowns and widely spaced cusps "to form a chopping mechanism." Carnivores had cheek teeth that formed "elongated, shearing blades" or robust, cone-shaped teeth for crushing bones. The teeth of insectivores such as shrews and hedgehogs had "cheek teeth with numerous sharply-pointed cusps." Humans have short, blunt, many-cusped teeth.

The single jaw hinge and musculature of mammal jaws also contribute to mammals' adaptability to many kinds of food sources. In mammals, jaw-muscle forces can be applied equally to either side of

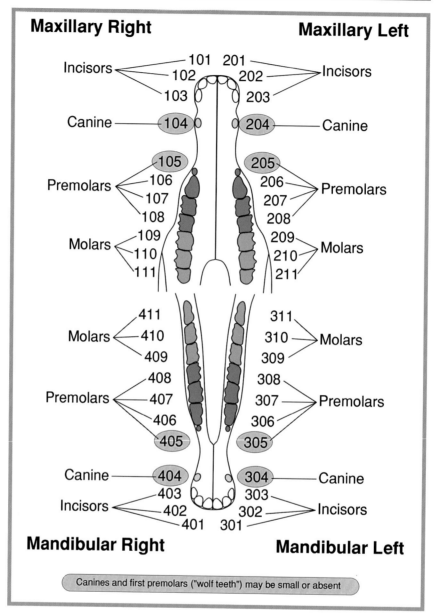

Maxillary Right   **Maxillary Left**

Incisors — 101 201 — Incisors
         102   202
         103   203

Canine — 104   204 — Canine

         105   205

Premolars — 106   206 — Premolars
         107   207
         108   208

Molars — 109   209 — Molars
         110   210
         111   211

Molars — 411   311 — Molars
         410   310
         409   309

Premolars — 408   308 — Premolars
         407   307
         406   306

         405   305

Canine — 404   304 — Canine
         403   303
Incisors — 402   302 — Incisors
         401 301

Mandibular Right   **Mandibular Left**

Canines and first premolars ("wolf teeth") may be small or absent

Paleontologists and zoologists use a grid called a dental formula to describe the kind and number of teeth found in the jaw. A dental formula for the horse is shown above.

the jaw; this ability vastly improves bite forces—and the accuracy of applying such forces—over what was available to mammals' reptilian ancestors.

Limbs, Posture, and Locomotion

Mammals moved away from the waddling, sprawling locomotion of their reptile ancestors by adapting many changes to the **appendicular skeleton**. Mammal-like reptiles, with their wide gait and dragging bellies, spent much of their energy merely lifting their bodies off the ground as they walked. There was a general transformation from the sprawling posture of reptiles to a more upright posture in mammals in which the limbs were positioned firmly underneath the body and muscle attachments migrated to a position high up on the limbs. Each of these adaptations improved the agility of mammals over their ancestors.

Kemp points out that having feet positioned closer together, underneath the body, improved the maneuverability of mammals and allowed them to make rapid changes in speed and direction and to traverse a greater variety of terrain with relative ease. Reptiles with a sprawling posture also drag their bellies, and some scientists argue that this prevents these reptiles from running and breathing at the same time. By lifting the belly from the ground, mammals improved their rate of respiration and were able to take full advantage of their active, endothermic physiology.

Places where the limbs connected to the skeleton—the hip and shoulder girdles—also were modified to allow for greater freedom of movement. This modification adds to the hypothesis that an upright posture made mammals more maneuverable than mammal-like reptiles. The rotating joints between the limbs and the shoulder and pelvic bones allowed for movement in long arcs and for great flexibility: No matter how fast, contorted, or stressed the body became, the limbs always were positioned beneath it for balance and control of locomotion. The bones of the pelvic region were fused to the vertebral column for added strength; this also aided locomotion. Movement of the limbs themselves was improved by more flexible knee and elbow joints that allowed the limbs to bend forward and backward, thereby conserving energy.

The organization of the vertebral column into specific functional regions was established in the earliest mammals. The vertebral column of mammals is another key to their posture, strength, and

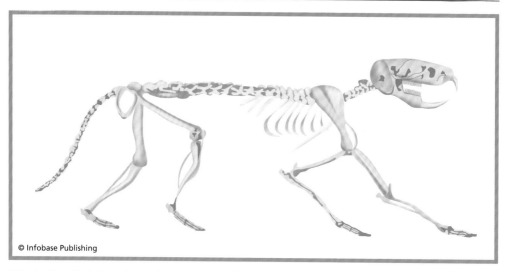

This is the skeleton of a vole, a very small mammal. The organization of the vertebral column into specific functional regions (neck, back, hip, tail) was established in the earliest mammals.

flexibility. Mammal vertebrae follow a consistent pattern, no matter how large or how varied the taxa. The skull is connected to the backbone by a ball-and-joint socket; this provides great flexibility in head movement. The vertebrae of the neck, called **cervical vertebrae**, number from six to nine and most commonly number seven. Even mammals with the longest or shortest necks have the same number of cervical vertebrae. In the giraffe, the seven vertebrae are elongated. In the whale, the seven cervical vertebrae are greatly compressed.

In mammals, the small ribs found on the cervical portion of the backbone are fused to the vertebrae, a trait that further improves the mobility of the head by providing a firm base to which neck muscles can be attached. The dorsal section of the vertebral column is associated with the back and contains ribs that protect the heart and lungs. As mentioned above, the hip bones are fused to the lower part of the backbone and provide a solid connection for the hind limbs.

Modifications to the hands and feet also improved the mobility of mammals. The inner finger or toe of reptiles was greatly reduced and not weight bearing; that inner digit became more stout and enlarged in mammals. The number of bones in the digits was also reduced; this simplified the structure of the digits while not sacrificing strength or flexibility. These small changes led to many varieties of mammal feet that were better adapted for grasping, walking, running, and climbing, whichever the preference might be for the taxa in question.

Brain Capacity and Senses

Unlike the relatively tiny brains of mammal-like reptiles, the brains of mammals increased in size enormously, even in the earliest taxa. Enlargement of the brain occurred in concert with the increasingly active lifestyle of mammals and was especially evident in areas related to sensory perception. Hearing was greatly improved by the modification of small bones in the rear of the jaw of mammal-like reptiles into the bones of the middle ear in mammals. Endocasts of brain cavities in fossil mammal skulls clearly show changes to parts of the brain devoted to **olfactory**, auditory, and visual acuity. This makes great sense for animals that could move faster and remain active longer than their reptilian ancestors. Whether a mammal was a predator or prey, it required more highly acute senses to improve its ability to survive.

The vertebrate brain has three basic sections: the forebrain, the midbrain, and the hindbrain. A tubular cord of nerves called the brain stem connects these three parts of the brain to the nervous system and spine.

The mammal brain retains many of its reptilian features and functions; it regulates such fundamental body functions as breathing and blood flow without having to engage the conscious mind. Evolutionary growth of the mammal brain has occurred primarily in the outer hemispheres of the brain; these areas show marked increases in higher-order thinking skills such as reasoning and speech communication. In addition to the enlarged sensory lobes found in mammals, the outer hemispheres of the brain—the "gray matter," or **cerebral cortex**—control the processing of sensations, the planning of actions and movement, memory, thought, and emotion. The portion of the cerebral cortex located in the forebrain is the conscious part of the brain. Located in the hindbrain beneath the cerebral cortex is the **cerebellum**, which controls body movement and became enlarged in mammals. The midbrain, including the brainstem, is responsible for sensory detection such as sight and hearing. Increased brain capacity was present even in the most primitive mammals, whose brain capacity, or volume, was at least four or more times the volume of the brains of basal amniotes.

Endothermy

Animals that create their own body heat and have a constant body temperature without regard to their surroundings have an endothermic, or "warm-blooded," thermoregulatory physiology. The activity level of an endotherm can remain constant in warm or cold weather. Reptiles are ectothermic, or "cold-blooded"; they absorb heat from their environment and cause their activity level to rise or fall based on outside temperature.

The evolutionary origins of endothermy in mammals are not well understood. It is difficult to ascertain the existence of an endothermic physiology directly from the fossil record. Instead, paleontologists rely on comparisons with extant mammals to accept that "warm-bloodedness" has been a crowning feature of mammals since their first appearance. Biologist Brian K. McNab has pioneered research into the question of the origins of endothermy in mammals. McNab believes that the development of endothermy may have been related to body size. There was a trend toward decreasing body size in the cynodonts, the direct ancestors of the first mammals. While certainly cold-blooded in origin, larger cynodonts could have maintained a constant body temperature because of their large mass rather than through an increase in their **metabolic rate.** During this phase of their evolution, cynodonts may have developed an insulating covering, such as fur, on their skin. Even as cynodonts evolved into smaller animals, argues McNab, the benefits of maintaining a constant body temperature, once gained, would not have been lost; it would have led to the first small mammals that happened to be fur covered and that began to adapt metabolic changes to regulate body temperature through endothermy.

The two basic functions of endothermy are, first, the maintenance of an elevated and constant body temperature and, second, the ability to sustain a high level of aerobic activity. Being endothermic is at the heart of being a mammal, and it comes at great expense. Thomas S. Kemp explains that the temperature physiology of mammals requires a tenfold increase in food requirements over their ectothermic counterparts—a cost that appears to have been balanced, in the evolution of mammals, by the benefits of endothermy: adaptability to more varied habitats, locomotory superiority, and higher brain capacity, all of which contributed to the dominance of mammals during the Cenozoic Era.

Other Physiological Systems

To enhance their survivability, mammals have adapted several other physiological traits and bioregulatory systems in addition to an endothermic thermoregulatory system.

Just as mammalian teeth have been adapted to process a wide range of food, so, too, has the mammalian digestive system. Mammals eat a wide variety of foods, from other animals of the sea and land to most conceivable types of plants. The majority of mammals are herbivores; these animals' digestive systems have adapted to extracting nutrients from cellulose, the primary component of plant cells. In addition to grinding plants to a pulp with their teeth, many large herbivores such as cows, giraffes, goats, and buffalo have four-chambered stomachs that act as fermentation vats. With the help of cellulose-digesting bacteria that live in the largest stomach chamber, these mammals pass food from one chamber to the next until the digestive system has thoroughly extracted the available nutrients.

Other herbivores—including rabbits, horses, and elephants—have a different kind of digestive tract. They, too, have friendly, cellulose-eating bacteria inside their digestive systems, but their stomachs consist of a single chamber only. This relatively small stomach acts mostly as a holding chamber from which food is passed through the intestines, where digestion takes place.

The circulatory system of mammals is driven by a four-chambered heart. Having evolved from the heart of synapsid reptiles, the

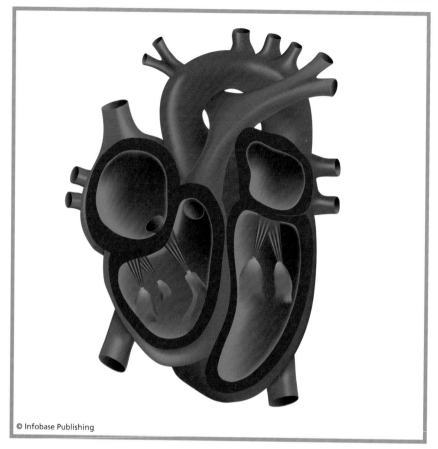

The circulatory system of mammals is driven by a four-chambered heart.

mammalian heart represents a continued adaptation of a system, seen in reptiles, for keeping the pumping circuits of the pulmonary and systemic systems separate.

The **pulmonary system** pumps deoxygenated blood out from the heart and passes that blood through the lungs, where a passive gas-exchange process removes carbon dioxide from the blood and enriches it with life-giving oxygen. The oxygenated blood is then pumped back to the heart. The **systemic system** pumps the oxygenated blood out from the heart to the organs and tissues of the body and then returns the oxygen-depleted blood to the heart to complete the circulatory cycle.

The mammalian circulatory system is similar to that of birds even though mammals and birds evolved independently from different sets of ancestors. Modern reptiles also have a dual circulatory system. A major difference between the mammalian heart and the hearts of birds and reptiles is that the mammal's circulatory system developed adaptations for nourishing the unborn fetus during its incubation period inside the mother's body. An organ called the placenta is the bridge, in mammals, for this exchange of blood nutrients, gases, and waste. It is a unique feature of mammals.

MESOZOIC MAMMALS

Only about 25 families of early mammals have been found in the Mesozoic fossil record. Some families are represented by no more than teeth; others are represented by remarkably complete skeletons. The fossil evidence is spotty and geographically biased, however, because of gaps in the availability of deposits bearing mammalian fossils of Mesozoic age. Considering that even dinosaurs are unknown from many spans of time during the Mesozoic, it should come as no surprise that the much smaller and less easily fossilized skeletons of early mammals are even scarcer. As a result, the evolutionary links that might join early mammal taxa are difficult to follow. This leaves great gaps in current knowledge about the roots of modern mammal families.

Chapter 4 will present a detailed classification scheme for modern mammals that includes all Cenozoic forms, living and extinct. For this discussion of Mesozoic mammals, it is important to introduce the highest levels of this classification now because some of the extinct members from the Mesozoic appear to be linked evolutionarily to modern forms. The broad group called Mammalia contains two major subgroups, the **Prototheria** and the **Theria**, as shown in the following figure.

The subgroup Prototheria ("first beast") includes mammals that lay eggs instead of giving birth to live young. The only surviving members of this clade are the platypus and the echidnas. Egg-laying

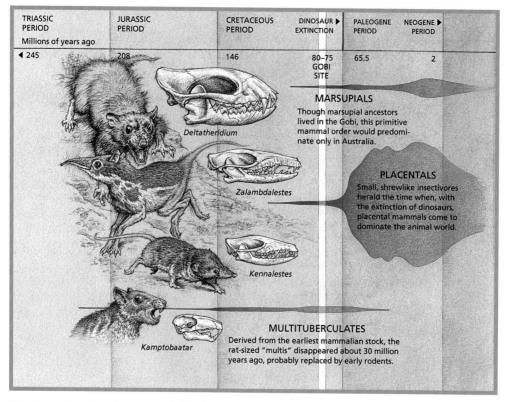

TRIASSIC PERIOD	JURASSIC PERIOD	CRETACEOUS PERIOD	DINOSAUR ▶ EXTINCTION	PALEOGENE PERIOD	NEOGENE ▶ PERIOD
Millions of years ago					
◀ 245	208	146	80–75 GOBI SITE	65.5	2

MARSUPIALS

Though marsupial ancestors lived in the Gobi, this primitive mammal order would predominate only in Australia.

Deltatheridium

PLACENTALS

Small, shrewlike insectivores herald the time when, with the extinction of dinosaurs, placental mammals come to dominate the animal world.

Zalambdalestes

Kennalestes

MULTITUBERCULATES

Derived from the earliest mammalian stock, the rat-sized "multis" disappeared about 30 million years ago, probably replaced by early rodents.

Kamptobaatar

The diversity of early mammals is shown in the variety of their skulls and teeth, each adapted for specific habits and food sources.

mammals also are called the **Monotremata**, or monotremes. The earliest known extinct members of this group date back to the Early Cretaceous Epoch.

The subgroup Theria ("true beast") includes mammals that give birth to live young. This large group includes two subgroups, the **Eutheria**, or placentals (after the placenta, a temporary organ found in females during the gestation of an embryo), and the marsupials ("pouch"), animals that also give birth to live young but whose reproductive traits differ from those of eutherians. Most of today's mammals are eutherians. Marsupials are found only in limited numbers today and are restricted to North America, South America, and Australia. They live in the greatest numbers and diversity in

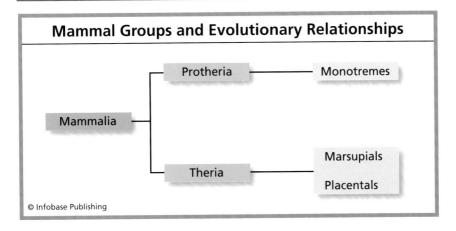

Australia. Eutherians and marsupials have roots in the Cretaceous Period.

The following is a summary of the best-known mammal taxa from the Mesozoic Era and the families to which they belonged. Some of these animals had descendants that persisted into the Cenozoic or even into the present time.

The First Mammals (Late Triassic to Early Jurassic)

The earliest mammals and their ancestors were small, probably endothermic, and likely nocturnal creatures. The shape of their teeth shows that they were probably insectivores that fed on small invertebrates.

Basal Mammals (Late Triassic to Early Jurassic)

Adelobasileus (Late Triassic, Texas). The provocative fossil specimen of *Adelobasileus* consists only of a partial skull that includes the braincase. This is enough to show, however, that this small creature had a brain that was larger than and modified over that of its reptilian ancestors. This places *Adelobasileus* intermediately between the cynodont mammal-like reptiles and the true mammals. Another term used for this kind of transitional vertebrate is a proto-mammal.

Sinoconodon (Early Jurassic, China). This is another basal proto-mammal that occupies an evolutionary position somewhat between that of the most derived cynodonts and that of the true mammals. *Sinoconodon* ("Chinese tooth") is known from a fairly complete skull and shows some of the same enlargement of brain areas that are seen in *Adelobasileus*. In addition, *Sinoconodon* has a fully formed single jaw joint and a more advanced inner ear than the cynodonts. In contrast to these innately mammalian features were *Sinoconodon*'s cheek teeth, which were more reptilian in nature and appear to have been replaced continuously throughout life. This tooth structure is unlike that of mammals, which have only two sets of teeth throughout life.

Morganucodonts (Early Jurassic)

Morganucodon (Early Jurassic, Europe, China, North America, and South Africa). The group of small, widely dispersed mammals known as the morganucodontids includes as its representatives the most complete specimens of early mammals. The lower jaw, or dentary, of *Morganucodon* ("Morgan's tooth") formed a single bone. The rear of the jaw had developed the single jaw hinge of mammals, and the remnants of reptilian jaw bones found in the rear of the jaw had become part of the middle-ear structure. Most importantly, *Morganucodon* had two types of teeth, premolars and molars. This represents an early stage in the evolution of the heterodont teeth of mammals.

Megazostrodon (Early Jurassic, South Africa). Like its close relative *Morganucodon*, *Megazostrodon* was a small quadruped and probably ate insects and other invertebrates, such as worms. The skeleton of *Megazostrodon* is the best known of such early mammals and reveals a body plan with a low profile but an erect posture. Measuring only about one-half inch (1.5 cm) long, this tiny mammal was most likely nocturnal and warm-blooded.

Indirect evidence for endothermy in *Megazostrodon* includes the presence of a secondary palate, a feature of the roof of the mouth. Paleontologist Michael Benton (b. 1956) suggests that, by separating the air path from the path occupied by the intake of food, this secondary palate allowed these animals to breathe rapidly while feeding. This feeding method is seen in many of the most active endothermic creatures today. In many other respects, *Megazostrodon* resembled

Megazostrodon (Early Jurassic, South Africa) was a small quadruped and probably ate insects and other invertebrates.

modern insectivores. Its nocturnal lifestyle is strongly suggested by its braincase, where enlargements to parts of the brain devoted to hearing and smelling are evident. Both senses are particularly helpful to nighttime creatures.

Hadrocodium (Early Jurassic, China). In 2001, the description of *Hadrocodium* by Zhe-Xi Luo of the Carnegie Museum in Pittsburgh and his colleagues provided yet another glimpse at early mammal evolution. *Hadrocodium* has been found in the same fossil locality as *Morganucodon* and *Sinoconodon*. *Hadrocodium* is an intriguing mosaic of primitive and derived features that, combined, illustrate yet another transitional phase in the evolution of reptiles to mammals. The specimen of *Hadrocodium* described in 2001 consists of an extremely tiny skull that measures only one-half inch (1.2 cm) long, nearly as small as the smallest known living mammal. *Hadrocodium* had teeth that were similar to those of *Morganucodon,* but several other features of *Hadrocodium* were more derived. These include the position of the middle ear bones, the jaw joint, and the larger size of *Hadrocodium*'s brain.

Triconodonta (Middle Jurassic to Late Cretaceous)

Members of the Triconodonta ("three-conical teeth") include early mammals whose molar teeth had a row of three main cusps, or points. Most triconodonts are known from tooth specimens alone, with the exceptions of *Jeholodens* and *Repenomamus,* described here.

Jeholodens (Early Cretaceous, China). That the relatively modern body plan of mammals was well established by the Early Cretaceous Epoch is suggested by the remarkable specimen of *Jeholodens.* This small mammal was recovered from the same fossil beds in Liaoning, China, that also have yielded wonderfully preserved small feathered dinosaurs and birds. *Jeholodens* was discovered in 1994 and described by paleontologist Ji Qiang of the Chinese Academy of Geological Sciences in 1999. It is just one of several remarkable mammal specimens that have added much to current thinking about the evolution of Mesozoic mammals. *Jeholodens* was a lightly built, slender mammal with a long tail. It measured about 2 inches (5 cm) long. The superficially shrew-like appearance of *Jeholodens* at first disguises some of its more primitive features. *Jeholodens* was a mosaic of modern and basal features. Its forelimbs and shoulder girdle were nearly modern and provided a more upright gait and great flexibility to the front of the body similar to what is seen in modern therians. Its hind limbs, however, were more reptilian and gave the back legs a decidedly sprawling gait.

Repenomamus (Early Cretaceous, China). Mesozoic mammals generally are pictured as exceedingly small (mouse-sized or perhaps rat-sized) creatures that ate insects, hid during the daytime, and were long overshadowed by their larger dinosaur contemporaries. This view changed in 2005, when a team of Chinese paleontologists headed by Hu Yaoming of the Institute of Vertebrate Paleontology and Paleoanthropology (Beijing) published its description of a large, ground-hugging, badgerlike mammal from the Early Cretaceous of China that measured about 3.3 feet (1 m) long. Even more remarkable was that this mammal, known as *Repenomamus* ("reptile mammal"), may have eaten young dinosaurs as part of its carnivorous diet. The excellent specimen of *Repenomamus* contains the remains of a tiny *Psittacosaurus* in the pit of its stomach area.

With a sizable jaw about the length of that of a fox, the mouth of *Repenomamus* was mostly lined with sharp teeth rather than molars. The animal had large, pointed incisors; large canines; and cheek teeth that could have been used to snag, hold, and rip apart prey. The back of the mouth included some blunt, molarlike teeth, but the stomach contents of the fossil specimen suggest that this animal did little chewing and instead swallowed its prey in large chunks. *Repenomamus* suggests that some lines of early mammals actually competed with dinosaurs for food and territory.

Multituberculates (Middle Jurassic to Late Eocene)
Multituberculates, now extinct, represent one of the longest-lasting branches of mammal evolution. Early members of this branch date back to the Middle Jurassic Epoch, and the last of the multituberculates became extinct 100 million years later, in the Late Eocene Period. The name *multituberculate* is derived from the nature of the animals' molars, which had multiple cusps, or "tubercles."

The multituberculates may have been the first widespread mammal herbivores. Some members of this group were **omnivorous**, probably were rodentlike in lifestyle, and ranged in size from about that of a mouse to that of a small groundhog. About 70 taxa of multituberculates have been described; most of these are from the Cenozoic Era. The fossils of multituberculates are some of the most abundant of all mammal fossils. According to Thomas Kemp, 75 percent of the mammal fossils found in deposits of the Late Cretaceous and Paleocene are of this clade.

Kamptobaatar (Late Cretaceous, Mongolia). This creature from the Late Mesozoic of central Asia is known from a relatively complete skull. *Kamptobaatar* was rodentlike and small; it measured about 4 inches (10 cm) long. The animal had a blunt snout, a broad skull, and eyes that may have faced forward. It had large incisors but was not a gnawing animal like modern rodents.

Kamptobaatar and other multituberculates had a jaw that moved back and forth horizontally. This allowed the upper and lower premolars to crush and slice the food that the animals brought into their mouths. *Kamptobaatar* probably used its large incisors to grasp plant matter and move it into the grinding plane of the teeth in the back of the mouth.

Cimexomys (Late Cretaceous, Montana, Wyoming, and Utah). Named after the Bug Creek Anthills in Montana, where the original specimen was discovered, *Cimexomys* ("bug mouse") was a tiny mammal that lived among dinosaur nesting grounds. A partial specimen described in 2000 included a nearly complete jaw; it is one of the best specimens for showing the variety of teeth found in a Mesozoic multituberculate. In the dentary, the long incisor is deeply rooted: The tooth's single root extends far back into the jaw bone. The first premolar is long and is heavily serrated for slicing vegetation. The back molars in the upper and lower jaws are strongly cusped for grinding food as the jaw slides from side to side in a slightly rotating fashion.

Why this did tiny mammal live among the nests of such behemoths as *Maiasaura*, a duck-billed dinosaur? Perhaps, like modern-day rodents, *Cimexomys* found advantages to living among communities of larger animals whose waste included perfectly good leftovers and whose presence provided excellent shelter from the surrounding world, where predators certainly loomed in greater numbers.

Early Monotremes (Early Cretaceous to Late Cretaceous)

Monotremes are the only egg-laying mammals. The name *monotreme* means "single opening." This is a reference to the use of a single body opening, the cloaca, for the functions of urination, defecation, and reproduction—a trait shared with reptiles. Modern monotremes are restricted to Australia and South America and consist of two groups that include the platypus and the echidnas. The more basal nature of their physiology suggests that monotremes were among the earliest therians, predating eutherians and marsupials. Direct links between these lineages have yet to be established with confidence, however.

Fossil remains of Mesozoic monotremes are mostly restricted to jaw fragments, but with this evidence, scientists have been able to set some definitive dates for the origins of this lineage. The lower-jaw molars of *Steropodon* (Early Cretaceous, Australia) bear a close resemblance to the molars in fossils of platypus specimens from the Miocene. About 10 jaw fragments of *Teinolophos* (Early Cretaceous, Australia) also have been found. These fragments represent an animal that may have been only about 4 inches (10 cm) long.

Basal Therians (Middle Jurassic)

The basal therians included early mammals that are believed to be related to the two extant groups of therian mammals: the eutherians, or placentals, and the marsupials. Some basal therians share traits of both eutherians and marsupials.

Asfaltomylos (Late Jurassic, Argentina). Fossil remains of Gondwanan mammals from the Jurassic Period are extremely rare. At the time it was described, in 2002, *Asfaltomylos* was the first Jurassic mammal specimen from South America. The specimen consists of a dentary bone with teeth whose shape suggests that *Asfaltomylos* might be thought of as a holotherian—an ancestor of both the prototherians and the therians. The occurrence of *Asfaltomylos* in the Late Jurassic strongly suggests that its ancestors originated earlier, in the Middle Jurassic, and that this family of mammals may have been prevalent in the Southern Hemisphere until it was displaced by multituberculates and triconodonts during the Cretaceous Period.

Fruitafossor (Late Jurassic, Colorado). *Fruitafossor* was a chipmunk-sized mammal that lived in the Late Jurassic. Known from an excellent specimen, this small mammal was described in 2005 by mammal paleontologist Zhe-Xi Luo. Luo noted that *Fruitafossor* had limb specializations for digging, a familiar feature of anteaters that arose many millions of years later, in the Cenozoic. The hollow teeth of *Fruitafossor* were also adapted for eating social insects such as ants and termites. This provides clues to a previously unknown mammal fauna with limb and dental adaptations that differed from those of other known Mesozoic mammals. *Fruitafossor* is not thought to be an ancestor of modern placental anteaters, but, rather, an offshoot of mammal evolution that evolved some of the same features independently.

Volaticotheria (Late Jurassic to Early Cretaceous)

Volaticotherium (Late Jurassic/Early Cretaceous, Mongolia). *Volaticotherium* ("winged beast") was an early gliding mammal that resembled, but was unrelated to, the modern flying squirrel. Gliding flight evolved independently several times in vertebrates, and this is the earliest appearance of a gliding mammal in the fossil record—an adaptation previously unknown in the Mesozoic. The fossil of *Volaticotherium* exists as a nearly complete but squashed individual. The three-cusped teeth of *Volaticotherium* probably were derived from the teeth of earlier triconodonts, but *Volaticotherium*'s teeth differed significantly from those of its ancestors.

Other differences between *Volaticotherium* and other Mesozoic mammals included elongated limb bones; a long, flat tail; and a furry flap of skin for gliding. An impression of this flap is clearly visible in the fossil specimen. *Volaticotherium* took to the air at about the same time as birds and long before bats. Its sharp teeth were suited to eating insects. When *Volaticotherium* was described in 2006 by a Chinese team of paleontologists led by Jin Meng, the evolutionary relationships of this gliding mammal were so unclear that it was placed in its own extinct family.

Early Marsupials (Early Cretaceous to Late Cretaceous)

Marsupials are one of the two major subgroups of Theria. These are mammals whose young are born as little more than embryos; these immature young usually must be suckled within the safety of a pouch. Marsupials probably are more closely related to the egg-laying monotremes than to placentals. Known marsupials have a tooth pattern that clearly distinguishes them from eutherian mammals: three premolars and four molars. Eutherians, by comparison, have four or five premolars and three molars.

Alphadon (Late Cretaceous, North America). Similar to modern opossums, *Alphadon* was an omnivore capable of eating a variety of food. Because *Alphadon* is known primarily from its teeth, its appearance is mostly a matter of inference because of the similarities of its teeth to those of living opossums.

Deltatheridium (Late Cretaceous, Mongolia). *Deltatheridium* was an early marsupial—an opossumlike quadruped with canine teeth that probably ate insects. *Deltatheridium* was discovered in the 1920s but was represented only by skull and jaw fragments. For many years, *Deltatheridium* was thought to be a basal mammal and perhaps ancestral to the marsupials. The discovery in 1998 of a new set of *Deltatheridium* fossils that included a growth series consisting of several excellent specimens of individuals allowed paleontologists to conclude that *Deltatheridium* was itself a marsupial.

The presence of this early marsupial in Asia during the Late Cretaceous suggests that marsupials originated in Asia prior to radiating to the Southern Hemisphere, where they became the dominant mammal fauna in some regions. *Deltatheridium* had a short snout and an opossumlike body. Because the new fossils showed a growth series, they revealed how the animal grew and lost teeth as it matured and so enabled paleontologists to draw close ties to the tooth development pattern of extant marsupials.

Early Eutherians (Early Cretaceous to Late Cretaceous)

Eutherians (placentals) give birth to young that have undergone an extended period of growth inside the body of the mother. The majority of modern mammals are eutherians. A recognizable tooth pattern in placentals includes only three molars and a distinctive cusp pattern. Many of the best fossils of Mesozoic eutherians come from North America and Asia. Asia is the likely starting point in the evolution of these animals.

Eomaia (Early Cretaceous, China). The oldest known eutherian mammal is *Eomaia* ("dawn mother"). Small enough to fit in the palm of one's hand, *Eomaia* was discovered in fossil lake beds of China that also are known for many exquisite remains of small, feathered dinosaurs; birds; plants; and the largest known Mesozoic mammal, the dinosaur-eating *Repenomamus*.

The oldest known eutherian mammal is *Eomaia* (Early Cretaceous, China).

Eomaia was found on a rock slab that also preserved the outline of its thick, furry coat. The animal was only mouse sized, about 6 inches (16 cm) long including its tail. It had long fingers and claws that could wrap around branches as it climbed; these fingers and claws made it highly specialized for this task. Although its teeth and limbs place *Eomaia* closer to the eutherians than not, its narrow pelvis suggests that its young were born quite small and perhaps not entirely as well developed as the young of later placentals. Clouding the picture further is the presence of an epipubic bone, a small node in the hip area that is used by modern marsupials to support their tiny young.

Zalambdalestes (Late Cretaceous, Mongolia). *Zalambdalestes* is considered a basal member of the eutherians and, with its long, upturned snout, probably resembled the modern shrew. This small quadruped had strong front legs and long hind legs much like those of the modern elephant shrew, which runs and jumps along the ground in pursuit of insects. *Zalambdalestes* was about 8 inches (21 cm) long, including its long tail.

INTO THE CENOZOIC

The foundations of modern mammal groups were well established by the end of the Mesozoic, even though mammals were not dominant, and their presence was not entirely obvious from the fossil record. Small mammals were quietly making their mark the world over; many were living their lives by night and hiding by day, literally overshadowed by the dinosaurs that lorded over their existence. The great diversity that would characterize the Age of Mammals is not entirely evident in the fossil record of the Mesozoic. Even so, while most mammals of the Mesozoic did indeed live in a world overshadowed by dinosaurs, interesting developments in mammalian evolution were taking shape across the globe.

Mesozoic mammals had successfully blended the best of the traits of the reptiles with a suite of new anatomical and physiological features, such as endothermy and heterodont dentition, that gave mammals access to a wide variety of food. Their mostly small stature gave mammals an advantage when it came to sustenance; their food requirements were small when compared with the enormous energy requirements of large dinosaurs. Some lost lines of mammals experimented with novel ways to move about: They glided from trees or crawled up them. A few mammals even grew to a size that allowed them to compete with dinosaurs for both food and territory—a drama that, because of the demise of the dinosaurs at the K-T extinction, would never be fully played out.

Chapter 4 explores the first phase of the blossoming of mammal life in the Cenozoic Era, a time during which mammals would come out of the dark to live large in a world filled with new opportunities for life—and equally compelling risks for survival.

SUMMARY

This chapter explained the traits that form the basis of modern mammal anatomy and traced the history of early mammals during the Mesozoic.

1. The first mammals arose during the Late Triassic Epoch and slowly diversified throughout the Mesozoic Era. These mammals were descendants of synapsid reptiles and most closely aligned to the cynodonts, or mammal-like reptiles, of the Early to Middle Triassic Epoch.

2. Evolutionary traits that led to the first mammals included modification of the reptilian jaw joint, formation of the bones of the middle ear, and endothermic physiology.

3. All true mammals have hair, have mammary glands, and are warm-blooded. Other traits of mammals that vary widely from group to group include the presence of heterodont teeth; upright posture; enlarged brain and sensory capacity; and pulmonary and digestive systems to support an active, endothermic lifestyle.

4. Only about 25 families of early mammals have been found in the Mesozoic fossil record. Many early mammals are known only from fossil teeth.

5. The group of animals known as Mammalia includes two major subgroups, the Prototheria and the Theria. The Prototheria are egg-laying mammals and are often called monotremes. The Theria are mammals that give birth to live young. This group includes two subgroups, the Eutheria, or

placentals, and the marsupials. Each of these subgroups differs in its reproductive traits.

6. The earliest mammals and their ancestors were small, probably endothermic, nocturnal creatures that ate insects.

7. The roots of the monotremes, eutherians, and marsupials can all be traced to the latter part of the Mesozoic Era. Several other basal mammal forms lived during the Mesozoic but became extinct; the most prominent of these forms were the triconodonts and the multituberculates.

8. Mesozoic mammals successfully blended the best traits of the reptiles with a suite of new anatomical and physiological features such as endothermy and heterodont dentition; this gave mammals access to a wide variety of food.

4

Mammal Families and Relationships

By the end of the Cretaceous Period, the roots of the three modern lines of mammals had taken hold. These were the egg-laying monotremes; pouched marsupials that gave birth to tiny, premature young; and the eutherians, or eutherian mammals, which carried their young inside the mother's uterus until they were more fully formed before birth. Some earlier lines of mammals did not make it to the end of the Cretaceous. The squirrel-like, insectivorous triconodonts—such as *Jeholodens,* from China—that once were so populous, were extinct by the Late Cretaceous. The rodentlike, omnivorous multituberculates, once the largest group of Mesozoic mammals, survived into the Cenozoic but lasted only until the Eocene Epoch.

After the extinction of the dinosaurs, mammals quickly diversified in the Cenozoic to fill ecological niches the world over. Immediately following the K-T extinction, Earth remained warm and inviting; this was a carryover of the rampant greenhouse environment that had begun in the Late Cretaceous Epoch. Subtropical climates almost reached the poles, and the world's forests became home to a rapidly divergent collection of birds, insects, and mammals.

The rapid evolution of mammals during the first part of the Cenozoic Era—the Paleocene and Eocene Epochs—grew from archaic roots of the mammal tree established in the Mesozoic Era. The resulting creatures were adapted for a warmer world—a world in which changing seasons were barely noticeable and vegetation was mostly lush and tropical. Although related to modern mammals, most of the first members of the Cenozoic Age of Mammals were strikingly dissimilar from today's familiar mammals.

This chapter introduces the major groups of modern mammals that emerged during the Cenozoic Era. These groups include the categories that will be explored in more detail in the remaining chapters of this book, *The Rise of Mammals,* and whose story concludes in another book in this series, *The Age of Mammals.*

THE MODERN MAMMAL GROUPS

The classification of mammals is a source of continuing debate among paleontologists. As Michael Benton points out, a traditional point of view bases the organization of mammals on transitional anatomical features that are clearly discernable in the fossil record. Among such physical evidence are important clues such as the development of the single jaw joint, the formation of the middle ear, and heterodont dentition in early mammals.

A contrasting point of view rejects ancient forms as being mammals by definition, instead labeling them as Mammaliformes, stages of evolution leading to modern mammals.

While the distinction between these two arguments is somewhat academic, the more traditional point of view, in which the origin of true mammals is traced back to early forms of the Mesozoic, is largely concerned with the linkages over time between extinct forms and modern forms. This is the point of departure taken in this book.

To recap vertebrate evolution, there are several biological features that distinguish mammals from other living amniotes. These include the following:

- the presence of hair
- mammary glands and the nursing of young
- dentition with different kinds of teeth and unique jaw structure and musculature for consuming a wide variety of plant and animal food

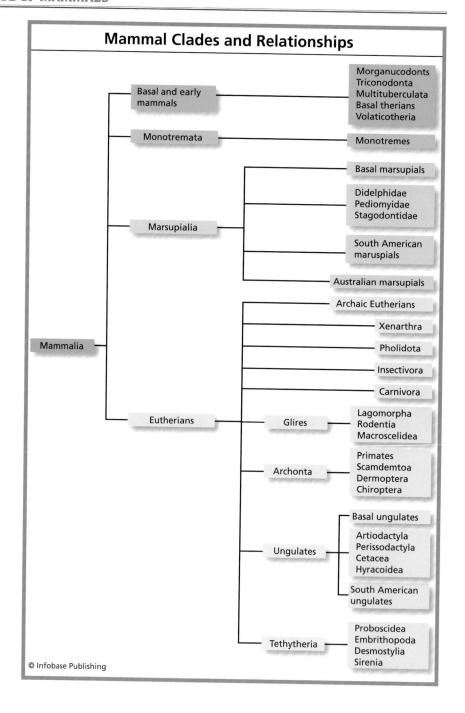

Mammal Clades and Relationships

Mammalia

- Basal and early mammals — Morganucodonts, Triconodonta, Multituberculata, Basal therians, Volaticotheria
- Monotremata — Monotremes
- Marsupialia
  - Basal marsupials
  - Didelphidae, Pediomyidae, Stagodontidae
  - South American maruspials
  - Australian marsupials
- Eutherians
  - Archaic Eutherians
  - Xenarthra
  - Pholidota
  - Insectivora
  - Carnivora
  - Glires — Lagomorpha, Rodentia, Macroscelidea
  - Archonta — Primates, Scamdemtoa, Dermoptera, Chiroptera
  - Ungulates
    - Basal ungulates
    - Artiodactyla, Perissodactyla, Cetacea, Hyracoidea
    - South American ungulates
  - Tethytheria — Proboscidea, Embrithopoda, Desmostylia, Sirenia

© Infobase Publishing

- upright posture and associated changes to the vertebral column, limb structure, pelvic and shoulder girdles, and musculature
- endothermic physiology
- large brain capacity and expanded sensory organs.

The anatomical changes that took place gradually over millions of years to form the mammalian line are clearly visible in the fossil evidence. Thomas Kemp describes the story of mammals as having three episodes. The first episode involved the Paleozoic origins of the amniotes and a subgroup of early reptiles that began to acquire mammalian traits by the beginning of the Mesozoic Era. The second episode was the firm establishment and early radiation of the first mammals during the Mesozoic. As the Mesozoic came to a close, all three extant lines of mammals had been founded: the monotremes, the marsupials, and the eutherians. The third and most dramatic surge in the development of mammals began after the K-T extinction and led to the great diversity of mammals that exists today. The major groups of Cenozoic mammals, some extinct, are illustrated in the accompanying diagram.

Multituberculates

The multituberculates entered the Cenozoic as one of the most successful lines of mammals but were extinct by the Eocene Epoch. Not part of the modern lineage of mammals, multituberculates nonetheless existed for more than 100 million years; this makes them one of the longest-lasting branches of the mammal family tree. Multituberculates had adapations similar to those seen in modern rodents and in most respects resembled such animals as modern squirrels, rats, and marmots.

Monotremes

The monotremes are the only extant group of egg-laying mammals. Only six species of monotremes still exist; all live in either Australia or New Guinea. The group includes the platypus and the echidnas.

Monotremes are considered the most primitive of living mammals, and at present their origins are poorly understood. The earliest monotreme fossils date back to the Early Cretaceous Epoch, and there is some thought that monotremes were part of an archaic branch of the mammal family tree that also produced the marsupials.

Marsupials

The marsupials are known for having a short gestation period and giving birth to tiny young that are barely more than embryos. Once born, marsupial infants crawl into the pouch of the mother, where they clasp a nipple and nurse for the balance of their infancy.

Living families of marsupials include opossums (North America and South America), kangaroos and koalas (Australia), and shrew opossums (South America).

Marsupials evolved at about the same time as eutherians; the two lines are unrelated other than to have a distant common ancestor. Cenozoic marsupials were confined largely to the continents of Australia and South America, where they diversified independently and became important components of the faunal assemblages of those isolated landmasses. The only remaining North American marsupial is the opossum, an offshoot of the South American marsupials. This North American offshoot is the result of an exchange of mammals first made possible about 3.5 million years ago, when a land bridge—the Great American Interchange—was formed between South America and North America.

Marsupials currently enjoy the greatest success in Australia, where there are as many as 175 species; this compares with about 75 species in South America and one in North America. Extinct marsupials from Australia are members of the clade Australidelphia; their South American counterparts belong to the clade Ameridelphia.

The success of marsupials in the Southern Hemisphere is due to the isolation of those continents during the early Cenozoic Era. Whereas placental mammals became the dominant mammal fauna in the Northern Hemisphere, marsupials reigned below the equator. The fate of many native South American mammal species, especially marsupials, was altered dramatically during the middle Pliocene, when the Great American Interchange allowed eutherians to migrate southward from North America and drive many native South American mammal species into extinction.

Eutherians

Eutherian mammals, whose young develop to an advanced stage prior to birth, make up the largest number of extant mammal taxa. Major groups of living and extinct eutherians are described below.

Archaic Eutherians

Several groups of early eutherian survived the K-T transition but became extinct in the early part of the Cenozoic. None of these groups has any clear descendants, but convergent evolution has resulted in some remarkable similarities to other mammal groups. The definitions of these groups are based on an evaluation of early mammal groups by paleontologist Thomas Kemp.

   Condylarthra. These were a group of extinct basal hoofed mammals from the early Cenozoic; they represent the early radiation of ungulates. The group probably was not descended from a common ancestor. Its members included small and mostly primitive herbivores, other herbivores that were significantly larger, and still others that were secondarily carnivorous.

   Creodonta. The extinct Creodonta lived from the Paleocene to the late Miocene and were the dominant carnivorous mammals for much of that time. Similar to, but unrelated to, the Carnivora, which arose at the same time, the Creodonta ranged across North America, Eurasia, and Africa and often achieved exceptional size, as in the African taxon *Megistotherium,* an animal that was the equivalent of a bison-sized tiger, at about 18 feet (5.4 m) long. The creodonts eventually were replaced in their ecological niche by the Carnivora, whose larger brains, more adaptable dentition, and foot structure gave them several advantages over the creodonts.

   Creodonts had relatively small brains for their body size; this implies that their senses may not have been as keen as those of carnivores. The creodont jaw had cutting cheek teeth set far back in the jaw. This made it more difficult for creodonts to consume anything but meat, whereas true carnivores have more varied dentition. This makes carnivores omnivorous and gives them more dietary options.

As for locomotion, creodonts had **plantigrade** feet; this means that these animals walked flat-footed, with the soles of their feet on the ground. Carnivores such as tigers and wolves are **digitigrade**: They walk on their toes. This makes them faster, quieter, and more agile than animals that must plant the flat of the foot on the ground with each step.

Palaeoryctoids. The Palaeoryctoids are known from North American fossils ranging from the Paleocene to Early Eocene, and their evolutionary connections are not well understood. The group is made up of insectivores. Some were shrewlike; others appear to have been burrowing creatures similar to moles. The Palaeoryctoids are known mainly from their distinctive teeth.

Anagalida. The Anagalida lived in Asia during the Early Paleocene. They were small omnivores with somewhat enlarged lower incisors and broad molars that were well adapted for eating vegetation. The anagalids are generally pictured as rabbitlike.

Mixodonta. This is another Asian group of small, probably omnivorous mammals with rodentlike incisor teeth. They lived during the Paleocene.

Pantolestida. The Pantolestida lived in North America and Europe from the Middle Paleocene to the Oligocene. They were otterlike, and through the course of their history they developed low, broad molars that some paleontologists believe were suited to eating mollusks.

Apatemyida. The Apatemyida lived in North America and Europe during the Early Paleocene and lasted until the Late Oligocene. Some taxa, such as *Sinclairella* (Oligocene, North America), had a mix of rodentlike and insectivore dentition, in this case resulting in a huge, single lower incisor that was somewhat spoon shaped.

Plesiadapiformes. Plesiadapiformes, including *Purgatorius* (Early Paleocene, Montana), were squirrel-like animals with strong climbing claws. They are found in North America and western Europe and had rodentlike dentition, with reduced canines and enlarged incisors. Some Plesiadapiformes were quite large for early mammals; one of these was *Plesiadapis* (Eocene, North America and France), which was about 12 inches (30 cm) long, including the tail.

Taeniodonta. The Taeniodonta included omnivorous tree climbers and diggers that lived in North America during the Paleocene and Eocene. The taeniodont body was stout, and the animals had powerful jaws equipped with chiseling canines and shearing cheek teeth. Taeniodonts ranged widely in size, from that of a rat to that of an opossum or a large boar.

Pantodonta. These were some of the first large eutherian mammals to appear in the Cenozoic. Early forms lived in China during the Early Paleocene, and the first occurrence of pantodonts in North America appears to have been in the Middle to Late Paleocene. Pantodonts often were dog sized, but they also represented the first large browsing mammals in the form of *Coryphodon* (Middle Eocene, North America), which was about 7.5 feet (2.25 m) long.

Tillodonta. Tillodonts were Paleocene herbivores with occurrences in China, Japan, and North America. Many tillodonts were small, although some taxa, such as *Trogosus* (Early Eocene, Wyoming), were bearlike in appearance, with rodentlike incisors, and grew to about 4 feet (1.2 m) long.

Dinocerata. These were the largest of the early Cenozoic browsing mammals but are disconnected evolutionarily from modern mammals. The group existed only from about the Late Paleocene to the Middle Eocene in Asia and North America. In their dentition, these often-large animals had reduced incisors but greatly enlarged canines. They once were thought to be related to the ungulates but now are thought to represent an unrelated lineage. Dinocerata probably had a lifestyle similar to that of the rhinoceros.

Arctostyopida. These were small, Late Paleocene mammals about the size of rabbits. They hailed mostly from Asia, with the exception of *Actostylos*, which was from North America. Arctostyopida had reduced canines and teeth of fairly uniform size.

Meridiungulata. The order Meridiungulata and five subgroups found within it represent a radiation of early (and now extinct) ungulates in South America. Lasting from the Early Paleocene to the border of the Pliocene-Pleistocene, about 60 million years later, this group originally was linked to North America but soon evolved on its own as the land bridge connecting the Americas disappeared during the Late Paleocene and Eocene. The origin of Meridiungulata might be connected to an ancestral line of condylarths from the Early Paleocene of North America, but the Meridiungulata soon diversified into their own characteristic groups.

South American ungulates evolved independently into some forms similar to those from the Northern Hemisphere; the South Americans included moderate to large herbivores similar to rabbits, horses, and camels. Other Meridiungulata were large, rhinoceros-sized animals. Some of these had trunks, tusklike canine teeth, and impressive batteries of plant-shearing cheek teeth.

Palaeanodonta. The Palaeanodonta date from the Late Paleocene and Eocene of North America. They were small but heavily built insectivores. Some of them, including *Metacheiromys* (Eocene, North America), appear to have been adapted to eating ants, although they probably were unrelated to the modern line of anteaters known as the pholidotans, which is described later in this chapter.

Glires

Glires includes the rabbits, the rodents, and the elephant shrews.

Lagomorpha. This group includes rabbits, hares, and pikas. Members of this group are jumpers; they also have four upper incisors that grow continuously and are worn down by the animals' continual feeding on vegetation.

Rodentia. This group includes mice, rats, porcupines, squirrels, woodchucks, and beavers. All rodents have an upper and lower pair of continuously growing incisors that must be gnawed down. This is the largest mammalian order in term of number of species.

Macrosceliddidae. This small group includes 15 species of elephant or jumping shrews from Africa. They are insectivores, and some species have long, trunklike noses.

Archonta

The Archonta include four seemingly different groups of mammals: tree shrews, flying lemurs, bats, and primates. Molecular gene analysis has upheld this group as having been derived from a common ancestor, although bats are further outside the group than the other members.

Primates. This group includes apes, monkeys, lemurs, gibbons, and humans. These tree and ground dwellers have large brains, **binocular vision**, opposable thumbs, omnivorous diets, and flexible limbs.

Scandentia. This group includes the tree shrews, which consist of 20 species that live in the tropical forests of Southeast Asia.

Dermoptera. The flying lemurs, or colugos, are gliding mammals that lead an arboreal life in Southeast Asia. There are only two known species.

Chiroptera. Bats are the only mammals to have evolved powered flight. Most are insectivores, but some species eat fruits, fish, or blood. Bats are nocturnal, travel by sonar, and make up the second largest category of mammals.

Ungulates

The ungulates include a variety of living and extinct hoofed mammal groups. Among the ungulates are the whales, which evolved from terrestrial hoofed mammals close to modern hippos.

Artiodactyla. These are the even-toed hoofed mammals, which first appeared in the Eocene. They include many familiar living mammals such as camels, pigs, hippopotamuses, deer, mountain goats, antelope, cattle, and giraffes. The weight of these animals is supported by the third and fourth digits of the feet; digits one, two, and five have been reduced or lost. These generally are browsing and grazing animals.

Perissodactyla. These are the odd-toed hoofed mammals. They arose in the Late Paleocene and are among the largest terrestrial mammals other than elephants. Members include horses, zebras, rhinoceroses, and tapirs. The third digit is weight supporting; in some taxa, such as the horse, it is the only remaining digit. Perissodactyls are browsing and grazing animals.

Cetacea. This group includes whales, dolphins, and porpoises. Cetacea have streamlined, nearly hairless bodies, and their forelimbs are modified into flippers. They breathe air. Some are toothed; others are toothless. As whales evolved from terrestrial hoofed mammals, possibly carnivores, they developed adaptations for making life possible in the water.

Hyracoidea. The hyrax group consists of four species of small mammals from Africa. About the size of a housecat, the hyrax is sometimes called the shrewmouse.

Tethytheria

The Tethytheria include the trunk animals (elephants), sea cows, and their relatives.

Proboscidea. This group includes the living and extinct elephants, mammoths, mastodonts, and their relatives. These animals are characterized by having a long, muscular trunk with one or two fingerlike appendages; incisors modified into tusks; and six cheek teeth on either jaw. They are the largest living land animals.

Embrithopoda. This is a group of large, extinct mammals from the Oligocene Epoch that grew large, bony horns on the **anterior** end of the skull. Their remains have been found in the Middle East and Central Asia.

Desmostylia. This is an extinct group of amphibious, hippopotamus-sized herbivores that lived during the Oligocene and Miocene of North America.

Sirenia. This group includes the manatees and the dugongs. The group is made up of rotund, nearly hairless aquatic herbivores with wrinkly skin and forelimbs modified into flippers. Other modifications for an aquatic life include a paddlelike tail, reduced hind limbs, and skull modifications that improve the animals' ability to gulp air and so hold their breath.

Xenarthra

Also known as the Edentata, the Xenarthra include the toothless insect eaters such as anteaters, sloths, and armadillos. The origins of these animals reach back 60 million years, to just after the K-T extinction. These taxa are called toothless because of their lack of incisors and canine teeth. Some have molar cheek teeth, although these are not well developed. The xenarthran hind foot has four toes, and the forefoot has two or three prominent claws; these are used to dig up insect nests and are specialized for climbing.

Pholidota

This family includes only one extant taxon—the pangolin, or scaly anteater—and eight species of scaly anteaters found in the tropics of Africa and Asia. Most pangolins are small, about cat sized, although the giant pangolin of Africa is about 4.5 feet (140 cm) long. The first pangolins date from about the early part of the Cenozoic Era.

Insectivora

This group consists primarily of small, burrowing animals: the moles, shrews, and hedgehogs. Insectivores probably have origins in the Late Cretaceous Epoch. Despite their primitive and unobtrusive nature, insectivores are the third-largest extant groups of mammals.

Carnivora

This group of mostly flesh-eating mammals arose during the early Cenozoic Era and remains the dominant predatory mammal group of today's terrestrial fauna. The senses of carnivores are keen, they have a large brain, and their cheek teeth have been modified into meat-shearing tools. Carnivores usually have three pairs of upper and lower incisors and prominent canine teeth. Terrestrial members of this group include dogs, cats, bears, weasels, and raccoons. Marine carnivores include sea lions, walruses, and seals. No carnivores are native to Australia, where marsupials took on the role of dominant predators.

EXPANDING HORIZONS

Mammals entered the first epoch of the Cenozoic having existed already for more than 140 million years. All three major lines of mammals that exist today had gained a foothold and had tread lightly, for the most part, in the nooks and crannies of a world otherwise dominated by larger predators that included dinosaurs, reptiles, and pterosaurs. Mesozoic mammals had adapted well to their "understudy" life: They had perfected endothermy; they had improved their sure-footedness; and they had developed a variety of teeth and muscular jaws that could process a wide variety of foods, including insects, vegetation, fruits, worms, and other small

THINK ABOUT IT

A Diversity of Rodents

Forty percent of all known mammal species belong to the group Rodentia, making rodents the largest single order of extant mammals by the number of living taxa. The name *Rodentia* means "to gnaw," a nod to the fact that rodents essentially have chewed their way into evolutionary history with their characteristically long, ever-growing incisors.

There are about 2,000 living species of rodents, and they live on all continents but Antarctica. Their success is attributed largely to their small size; their adaptability to a variety of foods (mostly vegetarian); and a short breeding cycle that allows them rapidly to increase the size of their **population**. Living rodents generally are small and include mice, rats, squirrels, chipmunks, dormice, mole rats, prairie dogs, hamsters, and gerbils. The largest rodents include beavers, porcupines, and the South American capybara, which resembles an overgrown guinea pig. Capybaras grow up to 4.5 feet (1.35 m) long and can weigh as much as 140 pounds (65 kg).

Modern rodents are not only populous but diverse. There are 43 species of flying squirrels alone, and they live throughout North America, northern Europe, Asia, and Southeast Asia. Rodents have adapted to most kinds of terrestrial habitats, from urban environments to forests, river basins, semitropical jungles, and desert plains.

Prehistoric rodents enjoyed no less diversity than living taxa and perhaps existed in even greater numbers than those seen today. According to recent molecular studies of fossil rodents, particularly by biologists Deborah Triant and J. Andrew DeWoody, some groups such as the voles animals. Some Mesozoic mammals had even become respectable predators and are known to have fed on small dinosaurs.

With the exit of the dinosaurs, new opportunities greeted the mammals. The largest of all plant eaters had disappeared and, along with them, the great predatory dinosaurs. Mammals were equipped

evidently developed new species 22 times more rapidly than did other kinds of mammals. That translates to one new species every 30,000 years instead of every 2.2 million years as seen in many other taxa.

Some noteworthy variations on the rodent theme included small horned rodents such as *Ceratogaulus* (Miocene, North America); the gliding mammal *Eomys* (Oligocene, Europe), a member of the same family of rodents that includes mice and rats; and *Castoroides* (Pleistocene, North America), a giant beaver that was about 8 feet (2.4 m) long. Although related to today's beavers, *Castoroides* had teeth that were less chisel-like and probably did a lot more chewing and grinding with its broader dentition. In addition, the tail of *Castoroides* was long and ratlike rather than wide and flat like that of a modern beaver.

The largest of all known rodents, living or extinct, was a giant guinea pig about the size of a small buffalo. *Phoberomys* (Late Miocene, Venezuela) measured about 10 feet (3 m) long and weighed up to 1,500 pounds (680 kg). It appears to have lived near the water, where it fed on tough river grasses and tried to avoid the snapping jaws of such large, predatory neighbors as crocodiles.

Phoberomys probably stood with erect legs to support its great weight—a posture similar to that of a cow—and probably was slow moving. *Phoberomys* weighed a thousand times more than today's typical pet guinea pig, and it is likely that its ponderous and bulky nature eventually led to its demise. *Phoberomys* lived, after all, in an environment where other large herbivores such as hoofed mammals could escape predators more readily.

to fill the voids left open by dinosaurs and quickly evolved and radiated to far-flung corners of the globe to do just that.

The story of the Cenozoic Era is largely one of new opportunities. It is, however, also a tale of a world torn apart geologically and of the consequences such changes had on evolution. Pangaea, the giant "supercontinent" that held together for much of the Mesozoic Era, remained somewhat connected during the early part of the Cenozoic. This allowed the widespread dispersal of mammal fauna to all parts of the world and explains the similarities of mammal fauna found in Europe and North America, in South America, and, to lesser degree, in Australia.

During the Cenozoic, the continents began to drift apart; they eventually separated by the middle of the Cenozoic. This left mammal fauna on newly isolated continents to develop on their own. Marsupials thrived in Australia and outcompeted placental mammals. The story was just the opposite in North America, where eutherian mammals reigned supreme. South America had a successful population of marsupials as well, until a temporary land bridge—the Great American Interchange—brought an invasion of eutherians from the north to change the faunal mix of South America forever. Chapter 5 explores the extinct members of the group Mammalia that arose during the rapid spread and evolution of mammals during the first part of the Cenozoic, the Paleocene Epoch.

SUMMARY

This chapter introduced the major groups of modern mammals that emerged during the Cenozoic Era.

1. The three major lineages of mammals—the monotremes, the marsupials, and the eutherians—had all been established by the beginning of the early Cenozoic Era.
2. After the extinction of the dinosaurs, mammals quickly diversified in the Cenozoic to fill ecological niches the world over, although mammals were also relatively diversified during the Mesozoic Era.

3. Monotremes are considered the most primitive group of living mammals. Only six species of monotremes still exist; all live in either Australia or New Guinea. The monotremes include the platypus and the echidnas.

4. The evolution of marsupials was most successful on the landmasses of Australia and South America, both of which became disconnected from the landmasses of the Northern Hemisphere during the Cenozoic. Consequently, Australian and South American faunas evolved in isolation during the major part of the Cenozoic Era, and developed specific morphological adaptations.

5. Eutherians, or placentals, are the most widespread and successful mammal group. Major subgroups within the placentals include Glires (rabbits, rodents, and elephant shrews); Archontans (primates, tree shrews, flying lemurs, and bats); Afrotheres (elephant shrews, hyraxes, golden moles, elephants, manatees, and their extinct relatives); Ungulates (hoofed mammals, marine mammals, hyraxes and Cetacea); Tethytheria (elephants, manatees, and their extinct relatives); Palaeorctoids (extinct molelike mammals); Xenarthra (anteaters and other toothless insect eaters); Pholidota (pangolins); Insectivora (moles and shrews); Condylarthra (extinct basal hoofed mammals); Creodonta (extinct meat eaters); and Carnivora (dogs, cats, bears, weasels, raccoons, sea lions, walruses, and seals).

6. The story of the Cenozoic Era is largely one of new opportunities, but it is also a tale of a world torn apart by separating continents and the consequences of such changes for mammal evolution.

SECTION FOUR:
EARLY CENOZOIC
MAMMALS

5

Conquest of the Mammals: The Paleocene Epoch

Paleocene is the name given to the first, brief epoch of geologic time that followed the extinction of the dinosaurs. The name *Paleocene* means "early dawn of the recent," a fitting description for a world that was recovering from the devastating K-T extinction. It was a period of recovery and struggle for many forms of life, but in the case of mammals it was more than that. Mammals not only found the new, warmer world to their liking, but also diversified and spread rapidly to fill many ecological niches left open for herbivores and carnivores alike.

Geologic spans typically are marked by significant events regarding the geology and climate of the world. In the case of the Paleocene, which was only about 10 million years long, the epoch began 65.5 million years ago, with the aftermath of the K-T extinction, and ended about 55.8 million years ago, with an upsurge of global warming. During a span of only a few thousand years, Earth's land surfaces and oceans attained their warmest temperatures for all of the Cenozoic. Even the temperatures of Arctic and Antarctic oceans rose to nearly subtropic temperatures, and marine sediments indicate that the temperature change extended from the surface to deep into the ocean depths. The cause of this sudden warming trend is not entirely understood, but it seems to have been related to vigorous and rapidly erupting mid-ocean ridges that discharged massive amounts of carbon dioxide and methane into the oceans. Excess ocean gases escaped into the atmosphere and generated a global-warming event.

For mammals, the Paleocene was a fruitful time of adaptation and radiation. Some major landmasses of the world were still connected, which allowed mammals to wander freely from North America to South America and from Eurasia to Africa, India, China, and possibly Australia. Within 10 million years, by the start of the Eocene Epoch, these land bridges would largely be gone, so the seeds of mammal lineages that still populate the major continents all were planted during the Paleocene.

This chapter explores, in the major groups of mammals known from the fossil record, the kinds of mammals that emerged during the Paleoncene. The fossil record is somewhat spotty for the Paleocene Epoch—especially when compared with the diverse fauna of the Eocene—but it provides a fascinating glimpse of evolution in action as mammals adapted many specializations to cope with the changing world.

EXTINCT PALEOCENE MAMMALS

A problem facing paleontologists who study the resurgence of mammals in the Paleocene is a shortage of fossil locations for this epoch when compared with later spans of the Cenozoic. The fossil record of Paleocene mammals is best known from North America and, to a lesser degree, from South America, Europe, and Asia, where sketchier evidence is found. There are very few clues to the lives of Paleocene mammals from Africa, Australia, India, and Antarctica.

Most Paleocene mammals can be characterized as being small and rodent- or squirrel-like. Many lines of larger and diversified mammals, including the Archonta (primates, bats, tree shrews, and flying lemurs); the Ungulates (the hoofed camels, horses, pigs, and ancestral whales); the Tethytheria (elephants, sea cows); and the Pholidota (pangolins) did not appear until the Eocene Epoch that followed.

The following is an overview of the best known extinct Paleocene mammal groups, organized according to the mammal classifications introduced in the previous chapter.

Multituberculates

The multituberculates had already been around for 100 million years by the time of the Paleocene, and they continued their success during the early stage of the Cenozoic. Multituberculates are distinguished for having been the longest-lived clade of mammals ever and for having survived the K-T extinction. While resembling modern rodents in many respects, multituberculates often combined traits seen in a variety of extant mammal families. Within this group were squirrel-like animals with **prehensile** tails and small, bearlike mammals with beaverlike heads. The multituberculates adapted to a variety of habitats. Some burrowed in the ground; some lived in trees; some were primarily ground dwelling; others may have been semiaquatic like modern otters or beavers. The pelvic bones of multituberculates are narrow; this suggests that these animals gave birth to their young early and that the mother needed to care for them for an extensive time.

Ptilodus (Early to Late Paleocene, western United States and Canada). *Ptilodus* was a relatively large member of this most successful group of mammals. Measuring about 20 inches (50 cm) long, *Ptilodus* was squirrel-like and is thought to have been a tree climber. Although *Ptilodus* had large incisors, close examination shows little abrasion between the upper and lower sets. This strongly suggests that *Ptilodus* was not a gnawing animal like modern rodents. Instead, the incisors appear to have been used for grasping food and moving it into the mouth. The most distinctive dental feature of a multituberculate was its long, thin, and striated premolars. With these premolars and a set of strong jaw muscles, the mouth of *Ptilodus* worked something like a nutcracker: The animal was able to secure large seeds or nuts and then crack them open by closing its powerful jaws. The tail of *Ptilodus* was long and probably prehensile. The animal's limbs were somewhat splayed, and it had a flat-footed stance. Noted mammal paleontologist Björn Kurtén pictured *Ptilodus* as having a low-slung, sprawling gait, a combination of lizard and squirrel.

Ptilodus (Early to Late Palocene, western United States and Canada) was squirrel-like and is thought to have been a tree climber.

Taeniolabis (Paleocene, New Mexico, Wyoming, Montana, and Saskatchewan). About the size of a modern beaver, *Taeniolabis* and its relatives were among the largest multituberculates. They had broad skulls and were equipped with powerful incisors for gnawing tough food. *Taeniolabis* lacked the large, bladelike premolars of *Ptilodus* and was too heavy to be a tree climber. It is believed that this large multituberculate was ground dwelling and possibly somewhat aquatic, like the beaver.

Monotremes: The Egg-Laying Mammals

The oldest known fossils associated with monotremes include teeth from Early Cretaceous deposits of Australia. The origin of monotremes is not entirely known, but most early fossils of these egg-laying mammals occur in Australia. *Monotrematum*, described here, provides evidence of the Early Paleocene presence of monotremes in South America, a remnant, perhaps, of fauna that interacted when the southern continents were connected as Gondwana during the last part of the Mesozoic Era.

Monotrematum (Early Paleocene, Argentina). Monotremes, the ancestors of the modern egg-laying platypus, are scarce in the fossil record until the Miocene and Oligocene, when the taxon *Obdurodon* is found. The earliest possible record of monotremes begins with *Monotrematum,* from the Early Paleocene of Argentina. *Monotrematum* is known only from a few teeth that resemble those of the platypus. Some paleontologists assert that *Monotrematum* is the same taxon as *Obdurodon*, although the larger size of the teeth of *Monotrematum* and a difference in age of nearly 50 million years suggest that the earlier taxon probably is a unique genus.

Marsupials: The Pouched Mammals

The best evidence of marsupials from the Paleocene comes from South America. The fossil record of North American Paleocene marsupials is scant, despite their known presence prior to the K-T extinction. Marsupials eventually would become the dominant mammalian fauna of Australia, but that evolutionary surge did not begin until the Miocene Epoch.

Early marsupials were the dominant insectivores of South America; these early marsupials also included small herbivores and respectably large carnivorous taxa. The Ameridelphia formed three major groups from the Americas: the small, opossumlike Didelphimorphia; the Paucituberculata, a clade made up of several groups of insect eaters, herbivores, and carnivores; and the Sparassodonta, a clade that consists of two groups of medium- to large-sized carnivorous taxa. All three clades had representatives in the Paleocene; examples are described below.

Pucadelphys (Early Paleocene, Bolivia). *Pucadelphys* was an early member of the didelphoid marsupials, small to medium-sized pouched mammals. *Pucadelphys* is well known from several skulls and skeletons. One of these is a nearly complete **articulated** specimen, perhaps of an animal that was trapped underground in a burrow in a flood. The dentition of *Pucadelphys* suggests an omnivorous diet of plants, insects, and possibly small vertebrates. The claws of *Pucadelphys* were best adapted for digging rather than for climbing, a distinction between basal opossums and extant species.

Mayulestes (Early Paleocene, Bolivia). *Mayulestes* was a sparassodont, a member of an extinct line of carnivorous marsupials that led to some fearsome taxa later in the Cenozoic, including the saber-toothed *Thylacosmilus* (Miocene-Pleistocene, South America). *Mayulestes* had the basic body size and form of an opossum, including a prehensile tale, but its skeleton presents an animal with an agile body, great mobility, and flexibility. The lifestyle of *Mayulestes* most probably resembled that of modern martens; *Mayulestes* probably scampered along the ground or across tree branches to attack small, squirrel-like mammals or to invade the nests of birds. *Mayulestes* is the earliest known member of this carnivorous marsupial group.

Epidolops (Middle Paleocene, Brazil). Paucituberculates were one of the most prevalent groups of Paleocene marsupials. *Epidolops* is an early member of this herbivorous group and is known from a well-preserved lower jaw. The incisors of *Epidolops* were somewhat reduced from those of other marsupials, and the second premolar formed a large, bladelike cutting surface for shredding tough plants.

Epidolops was probably about the size of a rat, with a slender snout, lightly built limbs, and a long, hairy tail. Modern relatives include the shrew opossums of South America, a largely carnivorous clan that subsists on earthworms and small vertebrates.

Eutherians: The Placental Mammals

Most modern groups of eutherian mammals had roots in the Paleocene, including the rodents, the insectivores, the carnivores, and the ungulates. The Paleocene belonged, however, mostly to several now-extinct groups of early eutherian mammals that helped establish the domains and lifestyle that led to the dominance of placentals on nearly every continent except Australia.

Archaic Eutherian Mammals

Mimotona (Early Paleocene, China). With a dental formula similar to that of early rabbits, *Mimotona* is sometimes considered to be ancestral to the Glires. It might represent an evolutionary transition between the small, Late Mesozoic mammals such as *Zalambdalestes* (Late Cretaceous, Mongolia) and true rabbits. *Mimotona* is known primarily from teeth and is known only from Asia. It was a small, omnivorous mammal with glirelike incisors.

Onychodectes (Early Paleocene, North America). *Onychodectes* is the most primitive known taeniodont, a group of small omnivores, some of which could grow to about the size of a medium-sized dog. *Onychodectes* was smaller, about the size of a stocky opossum. Each of *Onychodectes*'s jaws had two moderately large canine teeth followed by a set of leaf-shaped premolars and widely spaced molars for shearing and chewing plant food. *Onychodectes* had well-formed grasping claws on its feet that enabled it to climb trees. The forelimbs and hands were larger and stronger than the hind limbs; this suggests that *Onychodectes* also could have been a rooter or a digger. The tail was strong and may have been prehensile like that of a modern opossum. Thomas Kemp describes *Onychodectes* as a "very generalized" animal; this means that it was not highly specialized for tree climbing, digging, or walking about on the ground but was relatively good at all three. By the Middle Paleocene and Eocene, however, more specialized climbers, burrowers, and browsers had appeared, even among the taeniodonts; this led to the demise of such generalized animals as *Onychodectes*.

Psittacotherium (Middle Paleocene, North America). Among the mammals that most rapidly adapted to the absence of the dinosaurs following the K-T extinction were the taeniodonts. About the size of a burly German shepherd, *Psittacotherium* had a large, tall skull that measured about 10 inches (25 cm) long. The animal was equipped with strong jaws and massive teeth for grinding fruits, nuts, seeds, and other plants. The name *Psittacotherium* means "parrot beast"; the animal is so named because of its short face and the beaklike snipping capability of its over-large front teeth. With overly large canines and chisel-like incisors, *Psittacotherium* was a gnawing animal that could ingest tough plant food and then grind it with its small, blunt cheek teeth. *Psittacotherium* was a more advanced taeniodont than the generalized *Onychodectes*, as *Psittacotherium* shows increased specialization in its dentition for the processing of tough vegetation. Like *Onychodectes*, *Psittacotherium* probably was a rooter and digger. Because of its large, bulky size, *Psittacotherium* was unlikely to be found climbing trees.

Arctocyon (Early Paleocene, France). *Arctocyon* was an early condylarth. The condylarths were small and primitive omnivores, some of which adapted specializations for eating meat. The skull and entire **postcranial** skeleton are known for *Arctocyon*. It had a long and low skull and sturdy limbs but probably was not the most agile of creatures. It was about the size of a small bear and stood about 18 inches (46 cm) tall at the shoulder. Its dentition included robust canine teeth and bearlike cheek teeth. The lower canines were taller than the uppers and neatly overlapped when the jaw was closed. *Arctocyon* was not the swiftest predator of its time, so it probably subsisted mainly on berries and fruits and enjoyed the occasional opportunistic kill or scavenge of a dead animal. Condylarths are considered to be basal members of the hoofed mammal clades that led to horses, cows, and other modern families, but the precise links to these archaic mammals are not entirely known.

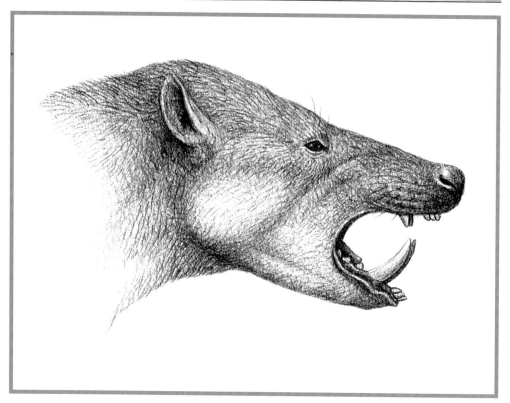

Arctocyon (Early Paleocene, France) was an early condylarth.

Meniscotherium (Late Paleocene to Late Eocene, North America). Condylarths made up the most plentiful radiation of plant-eating mammals during the Paleocene. They gradually edged out the multituberculates to become the first highly specialized plant-eating animals. With their more advanced teeth, which included crescent-capped molars more like those of modern deer and camels than like those of the multituberculates, condylarths feasted on leaves and fruits. Condylarths such as *Meniscotherium* represent one of the earliest successes for mammalian herbivores and omnivores. The evolution of some condylarths, such as *Meniscotherium*, exhibits adaptations similar to those seen in later, more advanced ungulates (hoofed mammals). These condylarth adaptations include hoofed toes and the shape and size of the animals' teeth. *Meniscotherium* was medium sized by condylarth standards; it was about the size of a beagle.

Titanoides (Late Paleocene, North America). Among the ground-dwelling mammals of the Paleocene forest were the unusual pantodonts, members of a group of early mammals that was well established in North America and Asia by the Late Paleocene. This group consisted of browsing animals that may have used their claws to uncover root plants, which they then ripped out of the ground with their large canine teeth. These heavy, five-toed animals could attain the size of a cow. *Titanoides* had a long, deep skull; muscular, heavy limbs; and a short tail. *Titanoides's* limbs were taller than those of its Late Paleocene relative, *Coryphodon* (Late Paleocene to Eocene, North America, Europe, and Asia). *Coryphodon* had a stout body and a more hippopotamus-like body plan. *Titanoides* may have had a partly aquatic lifestyle, using their upper canines like tusks to snag water plants.

Prodinoceras (Late Paleocene, Mongolia). *Prodinoceras* ("before terrible horns") is the earliest known member of the uintatheres, a subgroup of the Dinocerata that flourished during the Eocene. Like later members of the Dinocerata, *Prodinoceras* had reduced incisors but greatly enlarged upper canines. Its lower jaw and postorbital skull area showed the early development of flared bone surfaces that would characterize later dinoceratans, the skulls of which became adorned with a varied assembly of bones, nodules, and flaring protuberances. With its long, low, stout body, *Prodinoceras* was one of the largest of the archaic mammal herbivores of the Late Paleocene. It was about 10 feet (3 m) long.

Tytthaena (Middle Paleocene, North America). The Creodonta were an archaic group of carnivorous mammals that were the dominant predatory mammals of the Eocene and Miocene Epochs. Their beginnings are traced back to *Tytthaena* of the Middle Paleocene, a small insectivore about the size of a cat. Like other creodonts, *Tytthaena* had generalized dentition that was not as well adapted for processing meat as was the dentition of the true carnivores—the ancestors of modern cats and dogs—that were emerging at about the same time. Creodonts had larger incisors and canines, but Creodonta lacked the shearing and cutting edges on the premolars and molars that are found in members of Carnivora.

Glires: Rabbits, Rodents, and Elephant Shrews

Rodents and rabbits have in common a variety of derived traits, most notably their large, deeply rooted incisors and cheek teeth in both the upper and lower jaws. Rodents and rabbits have two such incisors in the lower jaw. In the upper jaw, rodents have two more incisors and rabbits have four. These gnawing and chewing teeth grow continuously and require the animals to put them to constant use. The earliest undisputed rodent fossil—*Paramys* (Late Paleocene and Early Eocene, North America)—appeared very late in the Paleocene; evidence for true rabbits begins in the Eocene. *Paramys* was first described in 1937 on the basis of fossil teeth.

Elephant shrews are small and mouselike, with large incisor teeth and high crowned cheek teeth. They are also distinguished by having pointed snouts and naked tails. The earliest elephant shrews, such as *Mylomygale* (Pleistocene, Africa) appear to be quite similar to extant species.

Xenarthra: Anteaters and Armadillos

The toothless anteaters, sloths, and armadillos have roots that take them back to the Paleocene. They apparently originated during that epoch in South America; this makes them perhaps the only group of extant mammals that first evolved on that continent. *Prostegotherium* (Late Paleocene, Brazil) was first described in 1902 and is one of the two earliest known xenarthrans, but little is understood about this animal other than its fossilized armadillo scutes, or body scales. Another xenarthran specimen was found in 1998 by a Brazilian team of paleontologists led by Lilian Bergqvist. Called *Riostegotherium,* this new taxon was found in the same fossil range as *Prostegotherium.* The fragmentary remains of two *Riostegotherium* individuals were identified. In addition to finding several scraps of body armor, the team recovered a few isolated limb bones that further reinforce the xenarthran affinity of the taxon. Not much more is known, however, so a more complete picture of this rare line of early mammals awaits additional discoveries.

Insectivora: Moles, Shrews, and Hedgehogs

While archaic forms of insectivorous mammals clearly were numerous during the Paleocene, the roots of the true Insectivora are less clear. These small, burrowing mammals include the burrowing and secretive moles, shrews, and hedgehogs. Insectivores are thought of as one of the most primitive groups among the living eutherians, but they are also one of the longest surviving.

Among insectivores, only the shrews have clear origins dating back to the Paleocene. The moles and hedgehogs followed during the Eocene. Among the earliest known shrews are related clusters of specimens from North America and Asia. These specimens are known almost only from fragmentary fossils of their teeth and jaws. *Leptacodon* (Late Paleocene, North America) appears to be the most basal member of the North American group; an Asian group that includes *Asionyctia* (Late Paleocene, China) and *Bumbanius* (Early Eocene, Mongolia) represents an offshoot of the North American branch. Little is known of the first shrews other than their dentition and jaws, which included sharp cheek teeth and large incisors.

Carnivora: Cats, Dogs, Bears, Weasels, and Raccoons

The Carnivora of the early Paleocene Epoch included primitive ancestors of today's dogs, cats, bears, weasels, and raccoons. These Paleocene Carnivora were not exclusively meat-eaters and were most certainly omnivorous in many cases. They did not grow to their famously large sizes until much later in the Cenozoic. Carnivores and meat-eating creodonts were distinguished from their insectivorous contemporaries by having pairs of upper and lower cheek teeth capable of shearing like scissors through meat when the jaw was closed. Members of the Carnivora had one set of such shearing cheek teeth on each side of the jaw. Early carnivores are placed in the groups Viverravidae—the early felines—and Miacidae—the basal canines.

Pristinictis (Early Paleocene, Canada) and *Pappictidops* (Early Paleocene, China) are some of the earliest members of the

Miacis (Late Paloecene to Middle Eocene, Europe) was an early carnivore related to dogs.

viverravids. These animals were the size of a small cat or weasel. They had slender, agile bodies; long skulls; and dentition that had adapted the early meat-shearing cheek teeth. Whether the earliest catlike carnivores were directly linked to modern families of cats, hyenas, and mongooses is a matter of debate. At the center of the discussion is the nature of the middle ear of the Early Paleocene cats. That middle ear differs significantly enough from that of other mammals for some paleontologists to assign the first catlike animals in a separate family for which there are no current representatives. Those scientists who prefer that line of reasoning trace the modern cats back to more recent fossil records from the Oligocene, about 30 million years ago.

Early carnivores related to dogs appeared later in the Paleocene and included such animals as *Miacis* (Late Paleocene to Middle Eocene, Europe). Members of the Miacidae were ferretlike animals that probably raced across the ground in search of smaller prey such as rodents and insectivores. Miacids differed from viverravids in that the miacids had a shorter skull and a modified ankle. *Miacis* had claws and limbs suitable for climbing trees or dwelling on the ground; this gave it an option to escape some of the larger, more agile ground predators of the time. From this early line of miasids arose the true weasels, dogs, raccoons, and bears.

TOWARD MODERN MAMMALS

The geographic disposition and climate of the Paleocene Epoch provided a platform for the launching of modern mammal families. Following the K-T extinction, mammals of many kinds diversified and expanded into numerous new ecological niches that were suddenly open to them. Mammals came out from hiding and became prominent participants in the evolution of life into new directions. The most ancestral mammal forms, carryovers from the time of the dinosaurs, continued to thrive and extended their reach in the trees and on the ground. Whereas an insectivorous lifestyle had dominated among the mammals that came into the Cenozoic, new mammaliforms arose during that era whose teeth and jaws gave them advantages in eating the abundant plant life that spread throughout the Cenozoic world. The first meat-eating mammals also arose during the Paleocene, first in the form of a carnivorous branch of the condylarths and then in the more specialized predators, the creodonts and the Carnivora.

Even though the Paleocene Epoch lasted only 10 million years—a mere minute or two on the face of the geologic clock—it was a momentous time of change for mammals. By the close of the Paleocene, the archaic mammals that dominated the Early Paleocene—including the multituberculates, condylarths, and pantodonts—were being replaced by early members of the modern mammal lines. Björn Kurtén calculated that about 22 percent of known mammal families became extinct at the end of the Paleocene, but this was by no means a disaster for mammals as a whole. The "new breed" of mammals was becoming more specialized to given habitats; this specialization allowed these new mammals to gain a stronger foothold than their predecessors. From this base emerged the extraordinarily diverse groups of modern mammal that continue to dominate the planet.

SUMMARY

This chapter explored, in the major groups of mammals known from the fossil record, the kinds of mammals that emerged during the Paleocene.

1. The fossil record of Paleocene mammals is best known from North America and, to a lesser degree, from South America, Europe, and Asia, where sketchier evidence is found.
2. The rodentlike multituberculates arose in the Mesozoic Era and continued through the Paleocene Epoch, thereby becoming the longest-lasting group of mammals. The multituberculates were beginning to dwindle by the end of the Paleocene; they were replaced by modern groups of eutherian mammals and became extinct in the Late Eocene.
3. The oldest known fossils associated with monotremes include teeth from Early Cretaceous deposits of Australia. Fossils of *Monotrematum* provide evidence of the Early Paleocene presence of monotremes in South America.
4. Paleocene marsupials were the dominant insectivores of South America and also included small herbivores and respectably large carnivorous taxa.
5. Archaic eutherian mammals were some of the most dominant mammals of the Paleocene; they include such groups as the taeniodonts, the condylarths, the creodonts, and the pantodonts.
6. Several modern groups of eutherian mammals had roots in the Paleocene. These include the glires (rabbits, rodents, and

elephant shrews); the xenarthrans (anteaters and armadillos); the insectivores (moles, shrews, and hedgehogs); and the carnivores (cats, dogs, bears, weasels, and raccoons).

7. By the end of the Paleocene, the extinction of archaic mammals had begun as those older forms gradually were displaced by modern mammal families.

8. The intense and brief global warming that marks the Paleocene/Eocene transition certainly favored intercontinental dispersion. According to current knowledge, several modern orders of mammals (cetartiodactyls, perissodactyls, and primates) appeared in the fossil record during this sudden global warming, and diversified afterward during the Eocene.

CONCLUSION

The Cenozoic Era marks the beginning of modern life. Following the K-T extinction, which closed the Mesozoic Era, the continents continued their separation, climates stabilized for a time, and life on Earth recovered. Many of the prominent geologic features seen today took shape during the Cenozoic.

Among the vertebrate survivors of the K-T extinction, birds and mammals were destined to become dominant terrestrial fauna. Modern birds, the Neornithes, were well positioned to expand their horizons in the Cenozoic. With an ancestral history linked to theropod dinosaurs, birds had devised a most successful biological plan to sustain their lineage. With roots in the Late Mesozoic, the first modern birds began their expansion with the ancestors of ducks. From there, bird taxa diversified steadily, if not instantaneously, to all parts of the globe.

Because of a lack of large terrestrial predators during the first part of the Cenozoic, several lines of giant, flightless, carnivorous birds arose by the Eocene Epoch. These included *Diatryma* in North America, *Gastornis* in Europe, and, by the Miocene, *Phorusrhacos* in South America. Mammals certainly were among these birds' frequent prey.

There currently are about 9,100 species of living birds in 153 families, plus an additional 77 known groups of extinct birds. Most of these modern bird groups arose during the Cenozoic Era—a testament to their longevity and adaptability.

For mammals, the Paleocene was a time during which they rose from relative obscurity and turned their insignificant early history into a solid foundation of evolutionary staying power. Snakes, lizards, crocodiles, amphibians, and fish held fast to the physiological adaptations that got them across the K-T extinction and have changed little even since that time. Mammals did just the opposite. They built on a highly adaptable biological formula and formed a succession of remarkably specialized variations that allowed them to take over many available ecological niches.

The evolutionary stages leading to modern mammal families were largely in place by the end of the Paleocene Epoch. The stages of increasingly derived features that make up modern mammals are summarized in the accompanying table.

EVOLUTION OF MODERN MAMMAL TRAITS

Trait	Early Appearance	Representative Taxa
Expanded brain and braincase	Late Triassic	Adelobasileus
Endothermy	Late Triassic	Megazostrodon
Erect posture	Late Triassic	Megazostrodon
Single jaw joint	Early Jurassic	Sinoconodon
Cheek teeth divided into premolars and molars	Early Jurassic	Morganucodon
Improved middle ear	Early Jurassic	Morganucodon
Loss of egg laying	Early Cretaceous	Sindelphys, Deltatheridium, Eomania
Triangular-shaped molars	Early Cretaceous	Aegialodon, Kielantherium
Longer incubation period in uterus	Late Cretaceous	Zalambdalestes, Barunlestes
Improved middle ear	Early Jurassic	Morganucodon
Hoofs replaced claws and nails	Early Paleocene to Middle Eocene	Meniscotherium, Dilododus, Hyracotherium

The success of the mammals can be attributed to many things: to their endothermic biology, which allows them the advantage of being self-energized and alert at any time of the day; to their superior dentition, which allows for the consumption of all manner of plant and animal food; to their enlarged brains and associated sensory prowess; and to an upright, flexible posture that provides maneuverability, speed, and agility as mammals navigate the various hazards that life has to offer. Yet another trait of mammalian biology might, however, provide an even greater advantage than those just listed: the mammals' reproductive strategy.

The history of vertebrate evolution has been marked occasionally by a significant change in the way vertebrates reproduce. Such a change usually has led to a spurt of increased diversification and radiation of species. When the first tetrapods became divorced from the water by laying their eggs on land, the change opened up an entirely new domain for vertebrates to conquer. The egg-laying strategy worked well for many millions of years and is still practiced by extant birds, reptiles, and amphibians.

Mammals improved further on the egg-laying reproductive strategy by incubating their young inside their bodies. This departure from egg laying also required that most mammals nurture their newly born young. A key to the mammalian reproductive strategy is the mammary gland. The milk-producing glands of mammalian mothers provide nourishment for newborn young, and the care and feeding of their young has proved to be advantageous to mammals.

The adaptation of nurturing the young might be related to the higher order of sophistication of mammalian biology. The intricacies of the mammalian body, brain, and physiological systems require more time to grow and mature than do the structures and systems of lower vertebrates. With such nurturing often come the additional benefits of behavioral development in the young. This development can be seen as young mammals follow the examples provided by their parents, who teach the young such basic skills as hunting, defending, foraging, and seeking shelter.

Mammal families established in the Paleocene experienced explosive growth during the next phase of the Cenozoic. The world of mammals prior to the appearance of humans is explored in the next book in this series, *The Age of Mammals: The Oligocene & Miocene Epochs.*

APPENDIX ONE:
GEOLOGIC TIME SCALE

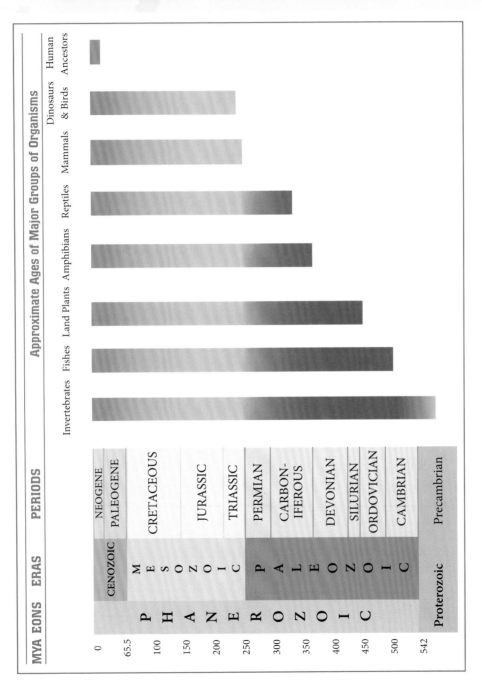

APPENDIX TWO: POSITIONAL TERMS

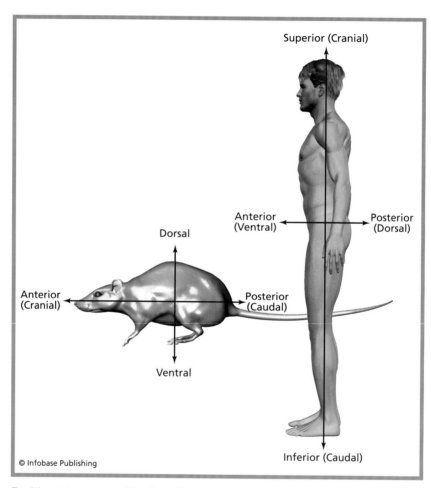

Positional terms used to describe vertebrate anatomy

GLOSSARY

adaptations   Anatomical, physiological, and behavioral changes that occur in an organism that enable it to survive environmental changes.

amniote   Vertebrate that produces an egg with a protective outer membrane or shell.

Anapsida   Vertebrate clade that includes all amniotes with a completely covered skull roof and no temporal fenestrae.

anatomy   The basic biological systems of an animal, such as the skeletal and muscular systems.

anterior   Directional term meaning toward the head, or cranial, end of a vertebrate.

appendicular skeleton   The part of the skeleton that includes the limbs and their shoulder and pelvic attachments.

archosaurian   A member of the branch of diapsid reptiles that includes dinosaurs, pterosaurs, crocodiles, birds, and their kin.

articulated   Condition of a fossil skeleton found with its bones in place, connected as they would have been in life.

basal   At or near the base or earliest level of evolutionary development; a term usually used to refer to an ancestral taxon.

bias   natural circumstances that favor fossilization, including the population, anatomy, size, and biology and habitat of a species.

binocular vision   Overlapping vision of the two eyes.

carnivorous   Meat-eating.

cerebral cortex   The outer hemispheres of the brain; the "gray matter" that controls the processing of senses, the planning of actions and movement, memory, thought, and emotion.

cerebellum   The part of the brain that controls movements of the body.

cervical vertebrae   Vertebrae of the neck.

clade   A group of related organisms including all the descendants of a single common ancestor.

climate   The kind of weather that occurs at a particular place over time.

coevolution   A change, through natural selection, in the genetic makeup of one species in response to a genetic change in another.

convergent evolution   Term used to describe a situation in which unrelated species each develop similar adaptations to similar environmental conditions.

dental formula   Numeric formula used to describe the kind and number of teeth in one half of the upper and lower jaw.

dentary   The lower jaw bone and its dentition.

derived   Term used to describe a trait of an organism that is a departure from the most basal (ancestral) form.

Diapsida   (diapsids) Amniotes with two temporal fenestrae, a lower one like the one seen in synapsids and a second one on top of the skull and behind the orbit.

digitigrade   Word used to describe tetrapods that walk on their toes.

dinosaur   Member of a clade of extinct ornithodiran archosaurian reptiles with an upright posture and either a saurischian or ornithischian style of hip.

disarticulated   Word used to describe a group of bones that are not joined or connected as they would be in life; disconnected fossil bones belonging to the same kinds of animals.

ectothermy   A "cold-blooded" thermoregulatory biology.

endothermy   A "warm-blooded" thermoregulatory biology.

era   A span of geologic time ranking below the eon; the Archean Eon is divided into four eras dating from more than 4 billion years ago to 2.5 billion years ago; the Proterozoic Eon is divided into three eras dating from 2.5 billion years ago to about 542 million years ago; the Phanerozoic Eon is divided into three eras, the Paleozoic, the Mesozoic, and the Cenozoic; the Paleozoic ("ancient life") Era lasted from 542 million to 251 million years ago; the Mesozoic ("middle life") Era lasted from 251 million to 65 million years ago; the Cenozoic ("recent life") Era began 65 million years ago and continues to the present.

Euryapsida   (euryapsids) Amniotes with one temporal fenestra positioned just above and behind the orbit.

Eutheria   Mammals that give birth to live young after an extended gestation period during which the embryo is nourished by means of a placenta, a temporary organ found in females during pregnancy; also called placentals.

evolution   The natural process by which species gradually change over time, controlled by changes to the genetic code—the DNA—of organisms and whether or not those changes enable an organism to survive in a given environment.

extant Term used to describe an organism that is living today; not extinct.

extinction The irreversible elimination of an entire species of organism because it cannot adapt effectively to changes in its environment.

fauna Animals found in a given ecosystem.

femur Upper leg bone.

flora Plants found in a given ecosystem.

forelimbs The two front legs of a vertebrate.

fossil Any physical trace or remains of prehistoric life.

gene A portion of a DNA strand that controls a particular inherited trait.

genera (singular: genus) A taxonomic name for one or more closely related organisms that is divided into species; names of organisms, such as *Tyrannosaurus rex*, are composed of two parts, the genus name (first) and the species name (second).

geographic isolation The isolation of species on a land formation as a result of naturally occurring geologic events (e.g., formation of an island or of mountains).

Gondwana Name given to Earth's southern landmass during the Mesozoic Era; formed by the breakup of Pangaea, Gondwana included regions that would become South America, Africa, India, Australia, and Antarctica.

herbivore An animal whose primary food source is vegetation.

heterodont Having different kinds of teeth in different zones of the jaw.

hind limbs The two rear legs of a vertebrate.

homodont Having similarly shaped teeth throughout the jaw.

ice age Periodic span of cooling that results in the development of ice sheets, or glaciers, that extend from the poles and that lower global average temperatures.

K-T extinction Mass extinction of the dinosaurs and other organisms that occurred at the boundary between the Late Cretaceous Epoch and the Tertiary/Paleocene Epoch.

Laurasia Name given to Earth's northern landmass during the Mesozoic Era; formed by the breakup of Pangaea, Laurasia included regions that would become the continents of North America, Europe, and Asia.

mammal-like reptiles A clade of synapsids that includes mammals, their relatives, and extinct ancestors; also known as Therapsida.

mammary glands   Milk-secreting glands of female mammals.

marsupials   Mammals that give birth to live young after a short gestation period; the newborn, immature young mature while being protected in an external pouch on the mother.

mass extinction   An extinction event that kills off more than 25 percent of all species in a million years or less.

metabolic rate   A measure of the combination of all biochemical processes that take place in an organism to keep it alive.

molecular time estimation   Computer-based method of determining the evolutionary age of a given taxon; molecular time estimation applies a known gene sequence and counts backward to estimate the origin of given traits and periods of speciation.

Monotremata   (monotremes) Egg-laying mammals; also known as Prototheria.

morphological   Pertaining to the body form and structure of an organism.

natural selection   One of Darwin's observations regarding the way in which evolution works; given the complex and changing conditions under which life exists, those individuals with the combination of inherited traits best suited to a particular environment will survive and reproduce while others will not.

Neognathae   A clade that includes all groups of modern, flying birds, living and extinct.

non-avian   A non-flying animal; term used to distinguish non-avian dinosaurs from birds.

olfactory   Related to the sense of smell.

omnivorous   Term used to describe an animal with a diet consisting of plants and meat.

Paleognathae   A clade that includes flightless birds, living and extinct.

paleontologist   A scientist who studies prehistoric life, usually using fossils.

Pangaea   Earth's major landmass that formed during the Permian and lasted until the end of the Triassic Period and that later broke apart into two smaller landmasses, Laurasia and Gondwana.

period   A span of geologic time ranking below the era; the Phanerozoic Eon is divided into three eras and 11 periods, each covering a span of millions of years; the longest of these periods, including the three in the Mesozoic Era, are further broken down into smaller divisions of time (epochs).

phylogeny   The family tree of a group of related organisms, based on evolutionary history.

physiology   The way in which an animal's parts work together and are adapted to help the organism survive.

plantigrade   Word used to describe tetrapods that walk flat-footed, with the soles of their feet on the ground.

pneumaticity   A morphological feature of the vertebrae of some dinosaurs; the vertebrae show concavities and sculpted spaces that lightened the body without sacrificing strength; pneumaticity may be related to the presence of air sacs throughout the body to distribute oxygen to tissues.

population   Members of the same species that live in a particular area.

postcranial   "Behind the head"; term generally used to refer to the portion of the vertebrate skeleton other than the head.

posterior   Directional term meaning toward the tail end; also known as the caudal end.

predator   An animal that actively seeks, kills, and feeds on other animals.

prehensile   Adapted for grasping or holding, as in prehensile tail.

Prototheria   Egg-laying mammals; also known as Monotremata, or monotremes.

pulmonary system   Part of the heart-based system for distributing oxygen through the body via the blood supply; in mammals, the pulmonary system pumps deoxygenated blood away from the heart and passes it through the lungs.

sacral vertebrae   Vertebrae that are fused to the pelvis.

species   In classification, the most basic biological unit of living organisms; members of a species can interbreed and produce fertile offspring.

synapomorphies   A derived trait shared by a group of closely related organisms.

Synapsida   (synapsids) Amniotes with one temporal fenestra positioned somewhat behind and below the orbit.

systemic system   Part of the heart-based system for distributing oxygen through the body via the blood supply; the systemic system pumps the oxygenated blood out from the heart to the organs and tissues of the body and then returns the oxygen-depleted blood to the heart to complete the circulatory cycle.

taxon   (plural: taxa) In classification, a group of related organisms, such as a clade, genus, or species.

temporal fenestrae   Openings, or "windows," in the vertebrate skull, just behind the orbit on the side of the skull, or temple region.

Therapsida   (therapsids) A clade of synapsids that includes mammals, their relatives, and extinct ancestors; also known as mammal-like reptiles.

Theria   Mammals that give birth to live young.

thermoregulation   The control of body temperature.

theropod   Member of a clade of archosaurs that includes all carnivorous, and some secondarily herbivorous, dinosaurs.

CHAPTER BIBLIOGRAPHY

Preface

Wilford, John Noble. "When No One Read, Who Started to Write?" *New York Times* (April 6, 1999). Available online. URL: http://query. nytimes.com/gst/fullpage.html?res=9B01EFD61139F935A35757C0A9 6F958260. Accessed October 22, 2007.

Chapter 1 – The Cenozoic Era

Berner, Robert A. "Atmospheric Oxygen Over Phanerozoic Time." *Proceedings of the National Academy of Sciences of the United States of America* 96, No. 20 (September 28, 1999): 10955–10957

Chumakov, N.M. "Trends in Global Climate Changes Inferred from Geological Data." *Stratigraphy and Geological Correlation* 12, No. 2 (2004): 7–32.

Dunham, Will. "Single massive asteroid wiped out dinosaurs: study." Reuters, December 1, 2006. Available online. URL: http://www. prisonplanet.com/articles/december2006/011206asteroid.htm Accessed March 5, 2008.

Ellis, Richard. *No Turning Back: The Life and Death of Animal Species.* New York: Harper Collins, 2004.

Kious, W. Jacquelyne, and Robert I. Tilling. *This Dynamic Earth: The Story of Plate Tectonics.* Washington, D.C: The U.S. Geologic Survey, 2001.

Morgans, Helen S., and Stephen P. Hesselbo. "The Seasonal Climate of the Early-Middle Jurassic, Cleveland Basin, England." *Palaios* 14 (1999): 261–272.

Palmer, Douglas. *Atlas of the Prehistoric World.* New York: Discovery Books, 1999.

Prothero, Donald R., and Robert H. Dott Jr. *Evolution of the Earth.* New York: McGraw-Hill, 2004.

Raup, David M. *Extinction: Bad Genes or Bad Luck?* New York: W.W. Norton, 1991.

Rees, Peter McAllister, Alfred M. Ziegler, and Paul J. Valdes. *Jurassic Phytogeography and Climates: New Data and Model Comparisons.* Cambridge: Cambridge University Press, 2000.

———, Christopher R. Noto, J. Michael Parrish, and Judith T. Parrish. "Late Jurassic Climates, Vegetation, and Dinosaur Distributions." *Journal of Geology* 112 (2004): 643–653.

Ross, Charles A., George T. Moore, and Darryl N. Hayashida. "Late Jurassic Paleoclimate Simulation—Paleoecological Implications for Ammonoid Provinciality." *Palaios* 7 (1992): 487–507.

Saltzman, Barry. *Dynamical Paleoclimatology: Generalized Theory of Global Climate Change.* New York: Academic Press, 2002.

Chapter 2 – The Birds Diversify

Benton, Michael. *Vertebrate Paleontology*, 3rd ed. Oxford: Blackwell Publishing, 2005.

Boles, Walter E. "Fossil Songbirds (Passeriformes) from the Early Eocene of Australia." *Emu* 97, No. 1 (1997): 43–50.

Fastovsky, David E., and David B. Weishampel. *The Evolution and Extinction of the Dinosaurs*, 2nd ed. Cambridge: Cambridge University Press, 2005.

Kumar, Sudhir, and S. Blair Hedges. "A Molecular Timescale for Vertebrate Evolution." *Nature* 392 (April 30, 1998): 917–920.

MacFadden, Bruce J., Joann Labs-Hochstein, Richard C. Hulbert Jr, and Jon A. Baskin. "Revised Age of the Late Neogene Terror Bird (Titanis) in North America During the Great American Interchange." *Geology* 35, No. 2 (February 2007): 123–126.

Mayr, Gerald. "A Tiny Barbet-Like Bird from the Lower Oligocene of Germany: The Smallest Species and Earliest Substantial Fossil Record of the Pici (Woodpeckers and Allies)." *Auk* 122, No. 4 (October 2005): 1055–1063.

Padian, Kevin, and Luis M. Chiappe. "The Origin and Early Evolution of Birds." *Biological Reviews* 73 (1998): 1–42

Chapter 3 – Early Mammals

Benton, Michael. *Vertebrate Paleontology*, 3rd ed. Oxford: Blackwell Publishing, 2005.

Dahn, Randall D., and John F. Fallon. "Interdigital Regulation of Digit Identity and Homeotic Transformation by Modulated BMP Signaling." *Science* 289, No. 5478 (July 21, 2000): 438–441.

de Muizon, Christian. "*Mayulestes ferox*, a Borhyaenoid (Metatheria, Mammalia) from the Early Palaeocene of Bolivia. Phylogenetic and Paleobiologic Implications." *Geodiversita* 20, No. 1 (1998): 19–142.

Kemp, T.S. *The Origin and Evolution of Mammals.* Oxford: Oxford University Press, 2005.

Kurtén, Björn. *The Age of Mammals.* New York: Columbia University Press, 1971.

Montellano, Marisol, Anne Weil, and William A. Clemens. "An exceptional specimen of *Cimexomys judithae* (Mammalia: Multituberculata) from the Campanian Two Medicine Formation of Montana, and the Phylogenetic Status of *Cimexomys.*" *Journal of Vertebrate Paleontology* 20, No. 2 (2000): 333–340.

Rauhut, Oliver W.M., Thomas Martin, Edgardo Ortiz-Jaureguizar, and Pablo Puerta. "A Jurassic Mammal from South America." *Nature* 416, (2002):165–168.

Raven, Peter H., George B. Johnson, Jonathan B. Losos, and Susan R. Singer. *Biology,* 7th ed. New York: McGraw-Hill, 2005.

Savage, R.J.G. *Mammal Evolution: An Illustrated Guide.* New York: Facts on File, 1986.

Trofimov, B.A., and F.S. Szalay, "New Cretaceous Marsupial from Mongolia and the Early Radiation of Metatheria." *Proceedings of the National Academy of Science of the United States of America* 91, No. 26 (December 20, 1994): 12569–12573.

Turner, Alan. *Evolving Eden.* New York: Columbia University Press, 2004.

———. *The Big Cats and Their Fossil Relatives.* New York: Columbia University Press, 1997.

Wallace, David Rains. *Beasts of Eden.* Berkeley: University of California Press, 2004.

Worthy, Trevor H., Alan J.D. Tennyson, Michael Archer, Anne M. Musser, Suzanne J. Hand, Craig Jones, Barry J. Douglas, James A. McNamara, and Robin M.D. Beck. "Miocene Mammal Reveals a Mesozoic Ghost Lineage on Insular New Zealand, Southwest Pacific." *Proceedings of the National Academy of Science of the United States of America* 103, No. 51 (December 19, 2006): 19419–19423

Zhe-Xi Luo, Alfred W. Crompton, and Ai-Lin Sun. "A New Mammaliaform from the Early Jurassic and Evolution of Mammalian Characteristics." *Science* 292, No. 5521, (May 25, 2001): 1535–1540.

Chapter 4 – Mammal Families and Relationships

Agusti, Jordi, and Mauricio Anton. *Mammoths, Sabertooths, and Hominids*. New York: Columbia University Press, 2002.

Benton, Michael. *Vertebrate Paleontology*, 3rd ed. Oxford: Blackwell Publishing, 2005.

Bergqvist, Lilian Paglarelli, Érika Aparecida Leite Abrantes, and Leonardo dos Santos Avilla. "The Xenarthra (Mammalia) of Sao José de Itaboraí Basin (Upper Paleocene, Itaboraian), Rio de Janeiro, Brazil." *Geodiversitas* 26, No. 2 (2004): 323–337.

Kemp, T.S. *The Origin and Evolution of Mammals*. Oxford: Oxford University Press, 2005.

Kurtén, Björn. *The Age of Mammals*. New York: Columbia University Press, 1971.

Meehan, T.J., and Robert W. Wilson. "New Viverravids from the Torrejonian (Middle Paleocene) of Kutz Canyon, New Mexico and the Oldest Skull of the Order Carnivora." *Journal of Paleontology* 76, No. 6 (November, 2002): 1091–1101.

Prothero, Donald R. *After the Dinosaurs: The Age of Mammals*. Bloomington: Indiana University Press, 2006.

Raven, Peter H., George B. Johnson, Jonathan B. Losos, and Susan R. Singer. *Biology*, 7th ed. New York: McGraw-Hill, 2005.

Rougier, G.W., J.E. Wible, and M.J. Novacek. "Implications of Deltatheridium Specimens for Early Marsupial History." *Nature* 396, No. 6710 (December 3, 1998): 459–463.

Savage, R.J.G. *Mammal Evolution: An Illustrated Guide*. New York: Facts on File, 1986.

Turner, Alan. *Evolving Eden*. New York: Columbia University Press, 2004.

———. *The Big Cats and Their Fossil Relatives*. New York: Columbia University Press, 1997.

Wallace, David Rains. *Beasts of Eden*. Berkeley: University of California Press, 2004.

Chapter 5 – Conquest of the Mammals: The Palescene Epoch

Agusti, Jordi, and Mauricio Anton. *Mammoths, Sabertooths, and Hominids*. New York: Columbia University Press, 2002.

Benton, Michael. *Vertebrate Paleontology*, 3rd ed. Oxford: Blackwell Publishing, 2005.

Kemp, T.S. *The Origin and Evolution of Mammals*. Oxford: Oxford University Press, 2005.

Kurtén, Björn. *The Age of Mammals*. New York: Columbia University Press, 1971.

Prothero, Donald R. *After the Dinosaurs: The Age of Mammals*. Bloomington: Indiana University Press, 2006.

Raven, Peter H., George B. Johnson, Jonathan B. Losos, and Susan R. Singer. *Biology,* 7th ed. New York: McGraw-Hill, 2005.

Savage, R.J.G. *Mammal Evolution: An Illustrated Guide*. New York: Facts on File, 1986.

Turner, Alan. *Evolving Eden*. New York: Columbia University Press, 2004.

———. *The Big Cats and Their Fossil Relatives*. New York: Columbia University Press, 1997.

Wallace, David Rains. *Beasts of Eden*. Berkeley: University of California Press, 2004.

Zhe-Xi Luo and John R. Wible. "A Late Jurassic Digging Mammal and Early Mammalian Diversification." *Science* 308, No. 5718 (April 1, 2005): 103–107.

FURTHER READING

Agusti, Jordi, and Mauricio Anton. *Mammoths, Sabertooths, and Hominids*. New York: Columbia University Press, 2002.

Benton, Michael. *Vertebrate Paleontology*, 3rd ed. Oxford: Blackwell Publishing, 2005.

Ellis, Richard. *No Turning Back: The Life and Death of Animal Species*. New York: Harper Collins, 2004.

Fastovsky, David E., and David B. Weishampel. *The Evolution and Extinction of the Dinosaurs*, 2nd ed. Cambridge: Cambridge University Press, 2005.

Gould, Stephen Jay, ed. *The Book of Life*. New York: W.W. Norton, 1993.

Kemp, T.S. *The Origin and Evolution of Mammals*. Oxford: Oxford University Press, 2005.

Kurtén, Björn. *The Age of Mammals*. New York: Columbia University Press, 1971.

Lambert, David. *Encyclopedia of Prehistory*. New York: Facts on File, 2002.

Lucas, Spencer G. *Chinese Fossil Vertebrates*. New York: Columbia University Press, 2001.

Palmer, Douglas. *Atlas of the Prehistoric World*. New York: Discovery Books, 1999.

Prothero, Donald R. *After the Dinosaurs: The Age of Mammals*. Bloomington: Indiana University Press, 2006.

———, and Robert H. Dott Jr. *Evolution of the Earth*. New York: McGraw-Hill, 2004.

Raven, Peter H., George B. Johnson, Jonathan B. Losos, and Susan R. Singer. *Biology*, 7th ed. New York: McGraw-Hill, 2005.

Savage, R.J.G. *Mammal Evolution: An Illustrated Guide*. New York: Facts on File, 1986.

Turner, Alan. *The Big Cats and Their Fossil Relatives*. New York: Columbia University Press, 1997.

———. *Evolving Eden*. New York: Columbia University Press, 2004.

Wallace, David Rains. *Beasts of Eden*. Berkeley: University of California Press, 2004.

Web Sites

American Museum of Natural History. Vertebrate Evolution

An interactive diagram of vertebrate evolution with links to example fossil specimens in the world-famous collection of this museum.

http://www.amnh.org/exhibitions/permanent/fossilhalls/vertebrate/

Australian Museum. Palaeontology

An extensive visual guide to Australian fossils, including mammals and human societies.

http://www.austmus.gov.au/palaeontology/index.htm

Bernard Price Institute For Palaeontological Research, University of the Witwatersrand, Johannesburg. Fossil Picture Gallery

The Bernard Price Institute for Palaeontological Research provides information for a wide variety of South African vertebrate fossils.

http://www.wits.ac.za/geosciences/bpi/fossilpictures.htm

Clowes, Chris. Paleontology Page

A privately compiled but exhaustive resource on many paleontology subjects, including a valuable look at the Burgess Shale fossils.

http://www.peripatus.gen.nz/Paleontology/Index.html

International Commission on Stratigraphy. International Stratigraphic Chart

Downloadable geologic time scales provided by the International Commission on Stratigraphy.

http://www.stratigraphy.org/cheu.pdf

Maddison, D.R., and K.-S. Schulz. The Tree of Life Web Project

The Tree of Life Web Project is a meticulously designed view of life-forms based on their phylogenetic (evolutionary) connections.

It is hosted by the University of Arizona College of Agriculture and Life Sciences and the University of Arizona Library.

http://tolweb.org/tree/phylogeny.html

Paleontology Portal. Vertebrates

A resource that explores early vertebrate life; produced by the University of California Museum of Paleontology, the Paleontological Society, the Society of Vertebrate Paleontology, and the U.S. Geological Survey.

http://www.paleoportal.org/index.php?globalnav=fossil_gallery &sectionnav=taxon&taxon_id=16

Public Broadcasting Service. Evolution Library: Evidence for Evolution

This resource outlines the extensive evidence in support of both the fact and theory of evolution; the site's approach is based on studies of the fossil record, molecular sequences, and comparative anatomy.

http://www.pbs.org/wgbh/evolution/library/04/

Smithsonian National Museum of Natural History. Kenneth E. Behring Family Hall of Mammals.

This Web site for a newly renovated permanent exhibit explores how all mammals, past and present, are related to each other by virtue of common descent.

http://www.mnh.si.edu/mammals/pages/educators/index.htm

Scotese, Christopher R. Paleomap Project

A valuable source of continental maps showing the positioning of Earth's continents over the course of geologic time.

http://www.scotese.com/

Virtual Fossil Museum. Fossils Across Geological Time and Evolution

A privately funded, image-rich educational resource dedicated to fossils. Contributors include amateur and professional paleontologists.

http://www.fossilmuseum.net/index.htm

PICTURE CREDITS

INDEX

ABOUT THE AUTHOR

THOM HOLMES is a writer specializing in natural history subjects and dinosaurs. He is noted for his expertise on the early history of dinosaur science in America. He was the publications director of *The Dinosaur Society* for six years (1991–1997) and the editor of its newsletter, *Dino Times*, the world's only monthly publication devoted to news about dinosaur discoveries. It was through the Society and his work with the Academy of Natural Sciences in Philadelphia that Thom developed widespread contacts and working relationships with paleontologists and paleo-artists throughout the world.

Thom's published works include *Fossil Feud: The Rivalry of America's First Dinosaur Hunters* (Silver Burdett Press, September, 1997); *The Dinosaur Library* (Enslow, 2001–2002); *Duel of the Dinosaur Hunters* (Pearson Education, 2002); and *Fossil Feud: The First American Dinosaur Hunters* (Silver Burdett/Julian Messner, 1997). His many honors and awards include the National Science Teachers Association's *Outstanding Science Book of 1998,* VOYA's 1997 Nonfiction Honor List, an Orbis Pictus Honor, and the Chicago Public Library Association's *"Best of the Best"* in science books for young people.

Thom did undergraduate work in geology and studied paleontology through his role as a staff educator with the Academy of Natural Sciences in Philadelphia. He is a regular participant in field exploration, with two recent expeditions to Patagonia in association with Canadian, American, and Argentinian universities.